To Larry Acker —
I hope you enjoy these
old stories.

CROSSINGS

STEPHANIE L. FOWLER

Arcadia Enterprises, Inc.

Copyright 2008 by Stephanie L. Fowler

All rights reserved.

Photography by Kristen L. Fowler
Maps by Jason Wheatley
Dust Jacket Design by J.P. Flexner
Editing by Christopher Klimas

Library of Congress Number 2007928722

ISBN 978-0-9703802-4-1

About The Publisher

Arcadia Enterprises Inc. was founded to help celebrate and preserve the uniqueness and historical significance of the people, places and environs of Maryland and the Eastern Shores of Virginia and Delaware. You are invited to explore current and future offerings at **www.buyarcadiabooks.com**.

Dedicated

to

You

Contents

Acknowledgments	ix
The Storyteller	1
The Curse of Franklin	7
And Justice For All	59
Sons of the Chesapeake	139
A Forgotten History	173
Ana's Story	219
Source List	279

ACKNOWLEDGEMENTS

Without the help and kindness of many people, this book would not exist.

First, I want to thank my family for their endless support of my writing: my parents, Bruce and Jacqueline Fowler, and my sister, Kristen. You accepted me for always having my head in the clouds and my nose in a book. You never made fun of my little poems and stories over the years. You gave me the courage to believe that I had something to say; you gave me the courage to write. For that, I will always be grateful.

I want to say thank you to my fiancé, Thomas Burt, for his unwavering support of this book and of me. You are a dream come true.

My grandparents, Elizabeth and Delbert "Bud" Fowler and Edward and Naomi "Mae" Tarr – thank you for your support and encouragement over the years. We lost Edward in 1995 and we lost Mae just prior to the publishing of this book. Mae: I know you're gone, but thanks for the newspaper clippings that you saved for more than sixty years. Rest well, E.T. and Mae.

I would also like to thank my aunt, Judy Howard, for her help with various research endeavors. Thanks to Mike Howard who spoke with me about the Chesapeake Bay. Kirk Mariner, a not-so-distant cousin and noted local author, also gave me good information about Virginia. I appreciate his willingness to share with me. To Ginger and Gary Marshall and Nodie Bunch, you might not be family, but you might as well be. Thank you for sharing your memories with me.

I owe a great deal of gratitude to Washington College and my professors for their technical advice and professional response to my work. The English department made my four-year stay at Washington a truly special time in my life. Specifically, I would like to acknowledge Richard Gillin, Kathy Wagner, Jacqueline Jones and Melora Wolff who was a visiting professor at the time. Recently, Joshua Shenk offered me some technical assistance. Also, I cannot forget the Sophie Kerr committee who gave these old stories about the Eastern Shore a chance. I'll never forget that.

Several people that I have interviewed throughout the past six years have now passed. I appreciated their willingness to share with me their experiences and memories. I remain thankful to Mabel and Garland Jones, William G. Kerbin, Jr., Ky Tyler, Dora Jester and Grace Skeeter.

This could not be a book about the Eastern Shore without the indelible insights of Scorchy Tawes, a true Eastern Shoreman. I had the pleasure of interviewing him on several occasions and I can say, without hesitation, that no one compares to him.

Other people that I would like to thank for speaking with me on these stories are Sudie and James Gatling, Charles Crippen, Jr., Melvin and Clara Harris,

Royce Nelson, Fran Dize, Merv Lowman, Leonard Brown, and the entire Lipic family. Thank you for telling your stories and for letting me into your lives. I hope that I have shared your words in the best possible light.

A special thanks to The Somerset Herald for letting me dig through their archives during the Spring of 2001. Also, thank you to the Board of Directors of the Sturgis One Room School Museum for allowing me to visit your museum and for allowing me to write the great history that you have saved.

Lastly, I must thank the following people for their technical assistance in the production of this book: Christopher Klimas, for his wisdom as an editor; J.P. Flexner, for his guidance on the creation of the cover artwork; Paul Flexner and Joseph Kulha, for their expertise in creating the technical components and files for printing; Jason Wheatley, for his excellent work on creating the maps for this book; and Kristen Fowler, for the photography used on the cover.

Again, thank you, to each person who helped me bring this book to fruition. This has been an incredible journey.

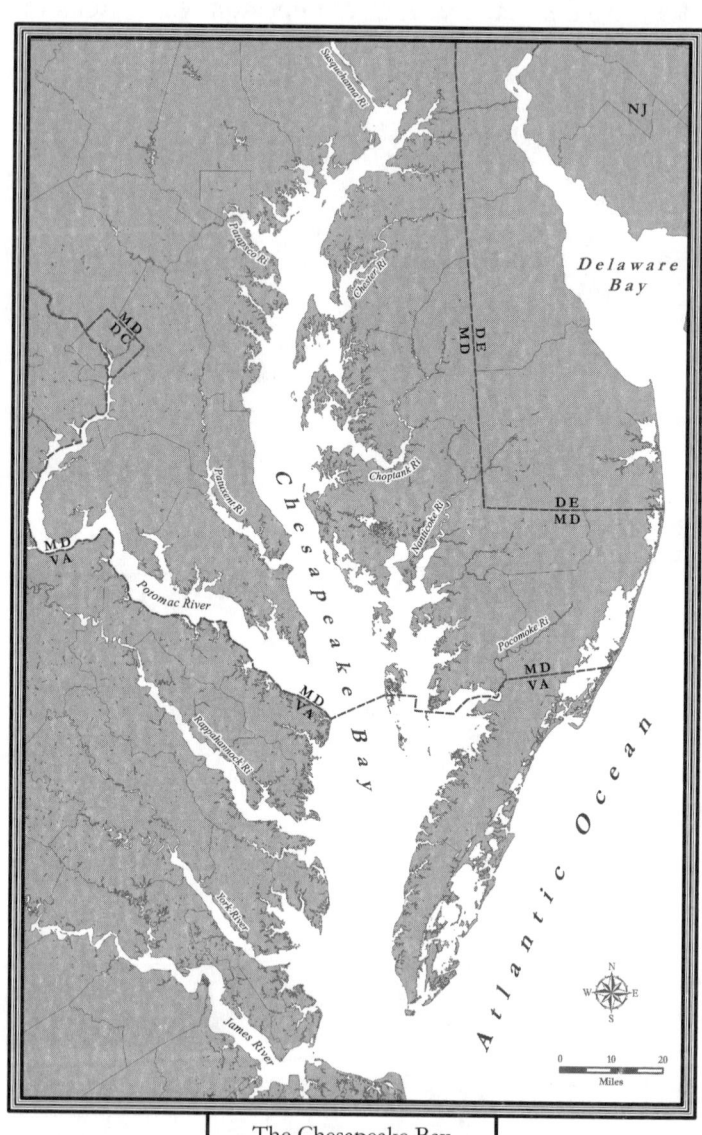

The Chesapeake Bay

THE STORYTELLER

Sit with me for a moment. I want to tell you a story.

Deep in the heart of this place, this congregation of three states, lies a simple truth. We are different. Perhaps it is our near-isolation from the rest of America that makes us this way. The Chesapeake Bay is a natural barrier to our west, though we have conquered her with a series of bridges and tunnels; to our east, we are cradled by the mighty Atlantic Ocean. Hundreds of rivers, inlets, and creeks cut into the peninsula from the bay and the ocean. For every man, woman, and child born here, the intimate understanding of the waters and the open spaces of land and horizon is a birthright.

That we are different should come as no surprise: being left to our own devices for so long created in us a wild independence and a stubborn defiance that cannot be broken. Our history has been strange and complex, full of scars and stoic moments. This is the place I call home and there are stories here that deserve to be remembered.

These stories are borne of old tales and nearly forgotten memories. The people that you will meet in the following pages are Eastern Shore folk, real characters who lived among the towns and harbors of our peninsula. They touched history, watched it, and in some cases, survived it. The towns carry few resemblances to what they once were. Progress and time tend to have that effect.

I have chased these wild characters and stories because I needed to capture the essence of something special, something larger than myself. In their rewriting,

I found my past, my present, and my future. I cannot escape my backwoods roots that bound me to tell these stories. Born and raised on the Eastern Shore of Maryland, I grew up with an instinctive respect for these lands and waters. Here, Eastern Shore people are neighbors, hard working and fiercely loyal. They are farmers and politicians, blue-collar and white-collar workers, waterman and small business owners. And although we may have our own misgivings and greed and pride concerning our Chesapeake and our lands, there is a desire to be exactly where we are. If we know anything, we know where home is.

Now, I must confess to you that I found great difficulty in narrating stories not borne of my own experience. It is a difficult task to maintain balance between the impulse to report the factual information and the desire to create a story. It is a difficult task to walk that line between fact and creative composition. Forgive me, please, if I jump inside of a character in order to tell a story that bears more than just facts, statistics, and linear map lines. Forgive me for imagining emotions and creating endings where, sometimes, none exist.

Here among the growing towns, marshy backlands, and anxiously awaited uncertainties, here where the Atlantic meets America is the home of our people. I have long nurtured a quiet fear that much of what I love about this place will be lost. Rich histories, weathered people, strange folklore – these are the natural resources of an Eastern Shore writer. Like sand, much of this is slipping through my fingers. The collection and preservation of these stories is vital to me because they are a part of who I am.

This Eastern Shore has an intrinsic hold on her people. Her tides dictate life, both in work and in pleasure. Her horizons are beyond beautiful: the sun is scattered for miles upon gold and green fields and dark waters. These scenes haunt me, following me into sleep, following me wherever I go.

All I ask is that you sit with me. Just for a moment.

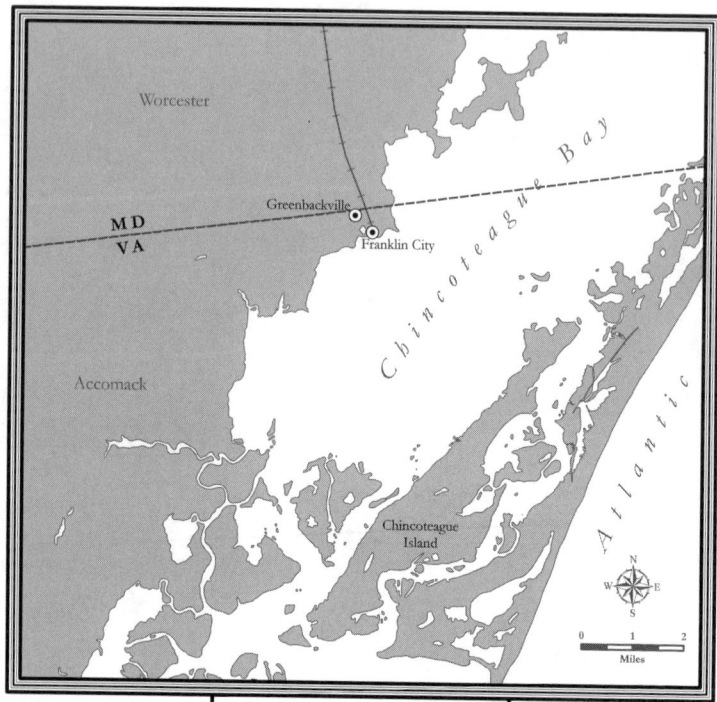
Chincoteague Bay, Virginia

THE CURSE OF FRANKLIN

As the sun sets on the Chincoteague Bay, nature slowly begins to retire from an exhaustive day of production. The tides calm their lapping on the shore and the sounds of the marsh animals reduce to low humming murmurs that drift above the grasses and trees and slip away over the water. Finally, there is peace, a nocturnal comfort that takes rest over the land while the sky begins another transition from blue to black. In those moments, something slips in between the salty reeds, brushing just slightly above the marsh and wills the air to stillness.

  I have seen and felt the strange quiet of sunsets on the Chincoteague Bay as my feet seemed rooted on the point of old Franklin City. There is a haunting here, and the echoes of unseen birds and the whisperings of winds that sneak around the rotting buildings speak of it all. The trauma lies silently exposed like the miles of oyster shells that lie heaped upon each other among old wooden pilings. Bleached white and worn smooth over time, these oyster remains reflect the sun like teeth or fragments of animal skulls. I have never stayed in old Franklin City after the sun disappears.

  As a child, I remember my mother told me one Halloween about a ghost town down in Virginia and she described the haunted, run-down houses, and the eerie sounds that came from those shores. My imagination ran absolutely wild. I already knew Franklin City long before I ever set foot on her remains.

  When I first saw the ghost village, I was much older, still a child but with older eyes. I learned that I was a descendant of its people. My grandfather, Edward Tarr was 22 when he worked as an oyster shucker in the port town of Franklin City. He earned a quarter for every gallon of oysters he shucked. Just up the road, less than a mile away, lies the modest town of Greenbackville, Virginia – the hometown of my grandmother, Naomi "Mae" Chapman Tarr. She attended the Methodist Episcopal Church in Franklin City. Her uncles and cousins owned some of the oyster shucking houses along the shores of Franklin City's beautiful bay. My grandparents met at the home of a mutual friend and were married in October of 1938. They were lifelong friends with another couple, Mabel and Garland Jones. Mabel was born and raised in Franklin City. They are just a few who outlived the town.

There is a haunting in the water and in the marshes, in the reeds and in the air. Something other than man rules this place now. Franklin City wants it that way.

Long before European explorers and settlers discovered these shores, Indian tribes had formed an intimate relationship with the land and waters. They knew the navigation of the creeks, guts, and inlet streams that cut the living landscape of pine trees, salt grasses, and brushing winds. The nomadic Indians of the peninsula, like the Nanticokes, Pocomokes, Gingoteagues, Assateagues, and Kicotanks, planted small fields of various crops, moving their settlements to new fields as the old ones gave out. They hunted waterfowl and harvested the shellfishes. The Indians instinctively held these lands.

With the settlements of Jamestown and others like it, it was only a matter of time before Accomack County would see settlers. In the late seventeenth century, a group of Virginians settled permanently on Chincoteague Island. In the decades to follow, the Indians moved closer to their neighbors while another history was being born. Not much is known of these Native American cultures because they were forgotten before they could be recorded. One can only imagine the peoples who once roamed these lands.

The first settlers of Chincoteague Island found that the soil was near perfect for cultivating crops, and the grasses were good enough to use as grazing pastures for animals. Early life on the island was nearly unlivable, yet they survived. Chincoteague remained a remote farming and fishing village for many years.

Long before the Civil War, the islanders began working the water and trading with the markets up North. When the South's passions intensified, Chincoteague Islanders overwhelmingly dissented with their Virginia brethren in seceding from the Union. Perhaps, trading with the North provided the small island with an economic security and the people of the island were loyal to the ideals that allowed them to survive and live on their own.

There is an old story that tells of a northern schooner captain who discovered the Chincoteague oyster boom of the late nineteenth century. It takes place in the early 1860s. The captain had been looking for oysters to sell in demanding northern markets and accidentally stumbled across the Chincoteague Bay. He skimmed the coast of the mainland and looked out over the land. The tall marsh weeds, standing erect, formed a dense wall at the waters edge. He couldn't see any dwellings or homes directly ashore. The water and land were so quiet that when the gulls cried, his heart jumped.

Still, the captain set about tonging for oysters. He found that the bay teemed with oysters of superior quality and he promptly filled his boat. As the old story goes, the captain went directly ashore to the nearest farm where he offered to pay the farmer $1.35 for each of the bushels of oysters he pulled up. The farmer readily agreed to the named price: a bushel of oysters usually went for fifty cents and rarely sold for more than seventy-five.

While the states' war raged on, the islanders and farmers on the mainland went on with daily life, virtually isolated from the tension and destruction. Farmers in that portion of Accomack County were beginning to make strong Virginian roots. The lands that would soon become Greenbackville and Franklin City were comprised of small farms. A man named Tull owned a majority of it in the early 1800s and he passed it down to his son. The village of Greenbackville began to emerge as one farmer, who owned most of the land, began to sell acres to other nearby people who wished to settle near the bay. By day, they made their way through the salt reeds, down to the water's edge, but by night, they were gone. For the villagers, the oysters of the Chincoteague Bay were as good as "greenbacks."

By 1863, merchants from New Jersey and Pennsylvania had already begun trading with the people of Chincoteague. Eventually, this partnership would become a full-time business operation. But the northern merchants and the people of Greenbackville and Chincoteague were not the only ones watching the bay with anxious, cashing eyes. Whispering reeds along the bank had seen a dark-eyed man move about the land. There was going to be a founding father to raise a city from the marsh.

John Rankin Franklin was a wealthy and prominent lawyer from Snow Hill, Maryland. A brilliant man and even better student, he graduated from Jefferson College at the age of 16 only to return home and join the faculty at the prestigious Washington Academy in Princess Anne, Maryland. He devoured law books and sought the tutelage of a notable Worcester County judge; by the age of 22, John Franklin had passed the Bar and set up his own practice. Just eleven years later, in 1853 he served as a member of the United States Congress.

But there was something about John R. Franklin that everyone understood and no one questioned. He could make things happen. Anything. If he wanted it, John Franklin would have it.

He, like many others, took a particular interest in the oyster boom. Early records indicate that the land had changed hands several times, and that John R. Franklin purchased more than two hundred acres from William and Sally Veasey. Perhaps not many men would have taken a liking to it, but John Franklin was a man of two laws: the Constitution and capitalism. He saw big profits and long-term income potential in the marshland because in the waters that washed up on the shores lay the oyster boom of the late nineteenth century. John Franklin did not think about the great storms of the past; he did not think about the sinkholes in the marsh. Cheap land and an oyster boom made for a bargain too hard to resist.

Abraham Lincoln's Union remained after the war and the impoverished South was left to discover its own industry and personal recovery. For the watermen of the Eastern Shore, industry meant seafood shipments to the North: places like Baltimore, Philadelphia, and New York. More than ever, oysters were in heavy demand

and the little villages of the Eastern Shore found the means to recover and prosper. Oysters were living monies sleeping beneath the surface of southern Atlantic waters.

John Franklin's career was also on the upswing. In 1867, the same year that little Greenbackville became a town, he was elected as Judge of the First Judicial District in Worcester County, Maryland. Now, Judge Franklin had the kind of power few men in the region had, and among the first of his priorities was to create his namesake, his legacy. He was the Judge. The whispering reeds were right – a city would rise on the Chincoteague Bay.

Over the next few years, workers came in from all over the region. The bay was as quiet as ever. Watermen begin talking deals and deeds with the Judge. The winds rushed through the salt reeds, down towards the Atlantic. Equipment began moving into the marsh. The nocturnal murmurs buzzed and grew louder. The process of change had only just begun.

But laying the solid roads on the wet marsh was a difficult task, more than Judge Franklin or the workers had bargained for. Each day, they fought with the land, trying harder and harder to force the roads and the Judge's town into existence. Each night, the marshes pulled the roads father down, creating maddening sink holes instead of sturdy, industrial roads. This infuriated the Judge as he saw his marshes turning into quicksand, seemingly on purpose. Judge Franklin could not let that stand.

Late one afternoon, as a storm was threatening off the coast, the workers decided not to risk getting stuck in the marsh turned quagmire. Judge Franklin watched them walk away. The wind picked up and pushed the sturdy frame of the Judge forward just a step. He whirled around, faced the bay, and roared: "Goddamn you all to hell!"

The wind stopped and the tide came forward.

"You'll listen to me yet. This is my town and come hell or high water, it will be built!" The Judge commanded the marshes to be strong and the waters to be fruitful.

Silence ensued. The storm that threatened never came and the roads eventually took a hard shape. And for a time, there was cooperation and peace. Judge Franklin's foolish mistake was almost forgotten.

The town was perfectly planned and geometrically designed. Three streets would run parallel to one another and terminate near the water's edge while five streets would intersect perpendicularly. Judge Franklin intended his town to be perfectly divided into more than twenty blocks, housing hundreds of homes and even more residents. Franklin City was a planned community in the post-Civil War area, and it was to make him rich.

JUDGE JOHN R. FRANKLIN

Judge Franklin began to sell parcels of land at $25.00 per lot. There was no shame in the high prices and the waterfront property was bought quickly. The tall reeds that guarded the shoreline were cut back and the rough, sandy beaches were exposed to the invading eyes of the townspeople. In their place, oyster companies rigged up a processional of shanty houses for seafood processing. Shells, useless and ugly, were tossed upon the exposed shoreline that welcomed the covering of calcified scales. Homes and businesses were erected on expensive marsh lots.

But the Judge knew that Franklin City needed something special, a unique selling point. Franklin City needed to be necessary to the local people and he knew just what to do to make that happen.

Judge Franklin was a powerful stockholder in the Frankfort and Worcester Railroad, and the lines of the local branch extended as far as Snow Hill, Maryland. With the purchase of the bay front property and his influence with the railroad company, he was able to court the Frankfort and Worcester line all the way down to his marshes. A railroad station was constructed on a wooden pier over the Chincoteague Bay, and thick rods were driven into the firmest portions of the land to bind the train tracks to the Judge's little town.

Within a few years, the Frankfort and Worcester line would become the Delaware, Maryland, and Virginia branch of the Pennsylvania Railroad. Once again, Judge Franklin was blessed with tremendous success – the little city was like a deep pocket of money and it all belonged to him. The town was built on ingenuity, reliable capitalism, and hard work. But the water and the land silently provided the means for the growth of this little town.

By 1876, the railroad was finished, tracks extending from far inland down to and over the choppy waters of the bay. This venture was the pearl in Judge Franklin's oyster. A post office was installed in the town, and the following year, a hotel was built to accommodate all of Franklin City's weary travelers.

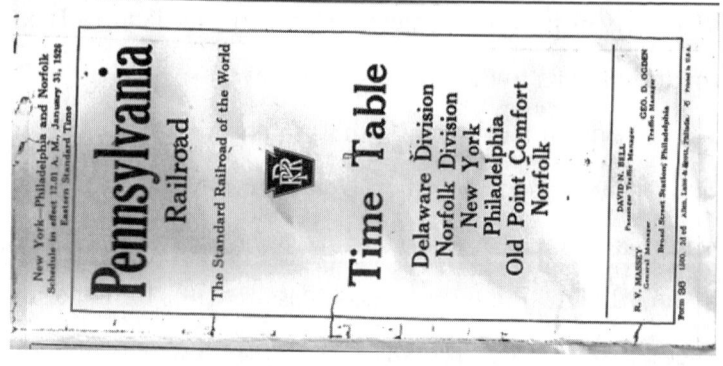

PENNSYLVANIA RAILROAD TIME TABLE CIRCA 1926
COURTESY OF MERVIN LOWMAN

With the completion of the railroad and with residents and merchants beginning to settle down, there seemed to be only one order of business left. The town was officially named in the Judge's honor. Boom or bust, Franklin City was born.

One year later, in the early winter days of January 1878, Judge John R. Franklin died at the age of 57.

Even though the Judge was gone, his town continued to prosper and serve the people of the region. With the train only seven miles away, the islanders of Chincoteague could export their goods with greater ease. This notion quickly became a reality as the first steamer, the *Widgeon*, cut the salt-water waves of the bay in 1885. By this vessel, a local minister traveled to Chincoteague Island one afternoon in 1886. He noted that he preached a sermon, married three couples, and baptized eight Methodists, and then rode the *Widgeon* home.

The *Widgeon* could make the trip across the bay in roughly thirty minutes, depending on the will of the water. This form of transportation allowed the mainlanders and the islanders to bridge a natural gap, to conquer seven miles of deep and often unruly water.

This man-made connection created an almost physical bond between the island and the terminus.

Chincoteague produce and seafood were carried across the bay in massive quantities to Franklin City where it was all packaged and loaded aboard northbound trains. The hungry markets were insatiable and the little villages like Franklin City, Greenbackville, and Chincoteague fed the frenzy as best they could. Oysters were plucked from the murky bay and quickly sold by the bushel and the barrel. Early figures are astonishing: during the late 1880's, more than 1,600 bushels of oysters left the shore each day by train and the year of 1888 saw the export of more than 33,000 barrels of oysters, selling for seventy cents per barrel.

And the oysters, to the delight of all, seemed never ending.

Marylanders and Virginians, including the Chincoteague Islanders, flocked to Franklin City to board the passenger trains and head off to exciting northern cities. Simply, it was the only place to see or to be seen. The little port town provided residents of the lower peninsula with access to the rest of the world. Ladies boarded trains to shop for dresses in Philadelphia and while they were gone, they could temporarily forget about their country homes in the remote, backwoods of the Eastern Shore of Virginia and Maryland. When they arrived at the depot, the men were waiting patiently for them: it was rumored that the men like to sit and watch as the women stepped off the trains because every now and then, one could catch a provocative glimpse of a lady's ankle.

Almost overnight, Franklin City boomed like few other towns before it. It was one of the most prosperous places in the county, the region even. In 1890, two trains a day made their way out of Franklin City. They brought in furniture, oil, and living necessities from the north and left carrying oysters and produce. One year saw the export of more than 50,000 bushels of potatoes. The dream of the late Judge Franklin was a reality: the roads were strong, the oysters were plentiful, and people were rushing in and out of the namesake town.

And time continued to pass. More people took up residency where the reeds used to stand and the marshes used to be free of train ties.

Nature, it seemed, was completely under the control of the people. The town was thriving on their will.

Yet no one seemed to notice the constant grinding of the train wheels on the wooden deck of the depot. The people of Franklin City seemed only to notice the fat and never-ending oyster harvests and the fashions, the lust and lure of all that came so easily. No one seemed to see the smoke smoldering on the bay. No one seemed to feel the swaying winds. No one understood.

Finally, on Sunday, May 23, 1896, someone saw the smoke.

Frank Price, a middle-aged engine operator, lived near the railroad depot. He had fallen asleep a little before midnight; nervousness had kept him awake. Frank was unsure about the cause of his anxiety. Something deep within him just would not settle. Finally, his tensions relaxed enough for him to drift off to a light sleep.

In the middle of the night, Frank opened his eyes and focused on a strange light in his bedroom. An orange glow cast itself on his wall. For a brief sleepy second, Price thought it was daylight. But then the bright shadow began to dance and change right before his eyes.

"Oh God, fire!"

He jumped from his bed and threw himself at the window: the railroad station was almost entirely consumed in a churning blaze. His home was so close to the burning depot he knew nothing could stop the fire from eating his house. All he could do was save himself and warn the others.

Frank ran into the streets of Franklin City, sounding the alarm bell. He was sure all the other homes near the depot would be destroyed as well. He rang the bell with all his strength and yelled fire until he was nearly hoarse. Within seconds, other residents were in the streets, all sounding a panicked chorus of "Fire! Fire!"

Telegraphing for help was not an option because there wasn't a machine in the town. Even if it had been available, no one could have arrived in time to save all the properties. Frank Price watched as his home was licked and teased by the fire and then consumed like an early course in a large meal. Frank Price's burning home provided the fire with easy access to the other homes and businesses on the west side of the railroad tracks. Frank felt absolutely helpless. Then something came to him.

"Hey, come with me. I have an idea," he yelled to a few men watching everything in the town burn. Frank took off running toward the roundhouse, shouting over his shoulder, "Help me get the first engine out. I'll go for help!"

The men did just as he told them. Smoke was filling the back portion of the roundhouse, and Frank urged them to be quick. The men worked hard and fast to get the engine and brave operator on the way to Stockton, Maryland to telegraph for help. But just as they cleared the roundhouse and boardwalk, the fire leaped onto the roundhouse and devoured it down to its wooden pilings anchored in the calm waters of the bay.

Winds raging in from the southeast pushed the flames over the edge of the roundhouse and onto the roof of a large storehouse of John F. Powell & Company, a major oyster company. The Powell storehouse erupted into flames along with the railroad yard, seven freight cars, and a passenger car.

From the storehouse, the fire spread quickly over the following hour, eating up every residence and business on both sides of the railroad tracks. One man, Bernard Powell of the very same oystering company that was on fire, did not wake up until the bed he was sleeping in caught fire. He grabbed his wife and a few articles of clothing and they escaped down the back staircase. Just as they made it out, the front roof collapsed.

Many others escaped only with their bedclothes and sought refuge in boats on the water. They watched from the bows of workboats and barges as the fire consumed their homes, their business, and their little city. The brilliantly laid out and perfectly designed town was nothing more than fuel for a glowing chaos.

As though God had decided to intervene, the only public building that was saved was the Methodist Episcopal Church. A vacant lot between the church and the last burning residence kept the fire contained. With no bridge for the fire to cross, the church survived. Slowly, the fire calmed to a slow burn and then, with no other homes or businesses to eat, the fire died next to the empty lot of the church.

The people came ashore like dirty sleepwalkers; their eyes wide and weeping, their feet bare with blackened soles, their faces broken and white like the thousands of shells awash on the shore. Some of the children cried and demanded to go home. They wished to be put in their safe beds and be left alone until morning. But there were no homes, no beds. The dirty sleepwalkers knew of only one place to seek solace – the church.

The minister put his arms around the congregation and together, inside the church, they prayed. They asked God for guidance and help. His will would be done, they agreed, and he would see them through this tragedy to better times. The children fell asleep on the pews that the parents had turned into makeshift beds. No one wanted to breathe – the smell of smoke permeated the church. That night, the women wept and men realized their ruin.

Outside, the tide retreated deep into the bay.

Word was sent from Stockton that a massive fire had destroyed Franklin City. The day after the fire, the main newspaper of neighboring Worcester County,

Maryland – <u>The Democratic Messenger</u> – ran the following headline: "Franklin City Swept Out!" Citizens from all over teamed up their horses and rode out to the bay to see for themselves the damages and the horrors recounted in their paper. When they arrived, they witnessed the smoldering ashes and charred remains of little Franklin City. All that remained: the church, three homes, and a few small oyster sheds.

The best estimates put the total damages at more than $50,000. The only portion of the damage that was covered by insurance was $25,000 worth of Pennsylvania Railroad cars. One man, Coard Chapman, recorded that he lost all of his furniture, but what he missed the most was his horse and cow, a personal loss of $1,000.

Franklin City was scorched, a burned out ruin, and its people were homeless and destitute. Residents of nearby Greenbackville turned out to support the victims of the fire, providing them with food and clothing, and the railroad company sent down a wrecking train to help with the aftermath and clean-up effort. Most of the homes were built on the water's edge, many on stilts in the Chincoteague Bay. These waterside homes were modest living quarters for many oystermen and their families. When the fire took the home, it took every possession. Many families were left with nothing at all.

The church provided the residents of Franklin City with shelter and food as well as hope and comfort. Local ministers asked their congregations to put together care packages to send to the destroyed town, and like good Christians, the people came together to help their brothers and sisters regain themselves after such an awful disaster.

Franklin City soon proved that it would not die so easily. The people worked hard and invested themselves deeply into rebuilding all the stores, oyster sheds, and homes. After a few months, Franklin City showed few scars of the burn. The trains were running back on schedule and the oyster companies were producing as many bushels of oysters as ever. More people were even building new homes along the main road and side streets. The town was recovering and conquering lost ground.

But in the marshes and along the shoreline, a recovery of a different kind slipped beneath the weeds and tides in search of a protective hibernation, a quiet place to hide.

Main St. Franklin City, Virginia

PHOTO OF FRANKLIN CITY, DATE UNKNOWN
COURTESY OF NAOMI TARR

By the turn of the century, life in Franklin City was booming. Almost 200 people lived in the town. The ferry service between Franklin City and Chincoteague was also growing. Another steamer, the *Chincoteague*, began traveling the seven-mile wide bay, and it was an amazing rig for all eyes to behold. The *Chincoteague* even had a side wheel. Back and forth the steamers would run, and Chincoteague Islanders were almost walking across the water. A few years later, the railroad company replaced the *Chincoteague* with a 69-foot gas powered tug named the *Broadwater*. All this meant was more prosperity and traces of oily slicks on top of the bay. The sludge swam down to the bottom of the bay, resting among the oysters. No one dreamed of the damage it might cause.

In 1908, a severe coastal storm pounded the little city for three days straight. Rain assaulted the homes of local oysterman and kept them from their daily runs in the bay. Businesses completely shut down; trains did not move; no one ventured outside where thunder shook the oyster shacks and lightning threatened every rooftop.

After the first night of heavy rains, the ground refused to soak up the excess water. By the afternoon of the following day, the streets of Franklin City lay under several feet of water. The ocean overtook the bay and invaded the homes of the townspeople. It stained everything with a muddy fingerprint that would not wash away. The waters kept rising, forcing residents to higher ground or at least, the upper floors of their homes. Doorsteps were sucked into the Chincoteague Bay as the storm reeled on its haunches and perched itself above the weather-beaten town.

After the third day of the storm, the rain slowly eased. The thunder quieted and the lightning was pacified to dull flashes in the evening sky. Over the next few days, the waters receded back into the bay and were swept back into the ocean. The townspeople began a massive cleanup effort, but the fingerprint would not be erased for many years.

Deep below the water, the hands of Franklin City had already grown too familiar.

Oysters were sold in several ways: by the barrel or by the bushel and either in the shell or shucked, meaning pulled out of the shell. Shucking oysters to reduce freight costs started in 1890; however, it became a widespread and popular practice in the early 20th century when oyster companies realized that they could reduce their transportation expenses and make higher profits by pulling the plump meat from the shell. Wooden shucking houses were built almost on top of one another as each company clawed at the bay to pull in more and more oysters.

For the bay, repeated harvests took the shape of relentless rapes, and as a result, the oyster population took a sharp decrease in 1915. What had once been so fertile and unyielding was showing signs of emaciation and disease. Most residents of Franklin City and

Greenbackville took to clamming during the summer, but the pay simply did not compare to oystering. Chincoteague Island was still producing farm goods and seafood, and Franklin City began to lean on Chincoteague's imports. A canning factory was established near the wharf and was connected to the roundhouse by a boardwalk on stilts. The factory workers skinned and canned fresh tomatoes and hurried them down wooden planks for loading onto the northbound trains. At the end of the day, all the tomato skins were emptied out into the open waters. By quitting time, the bay looked as though it were bleeding in the salt reeds.

The bay would take its revenge in 1918 as another flood wiped out the streets of Franklin City. For days, the residents took refuge in their attics and on their rooftops. Not one oyster was shucked and not one red tomato was skinned. The storm raged, and this time, the muddy fingerprint was larger and dirtier; the warnings had been delivered.

Franklin City's residents renovated or rebuilt the damaged properties and congratulated themselves on being a strong race of people. An integral part of living so close to the water is an inherent understanding of nature's untamed ways. Survival, they believed, was in their blood. It had to be – survival was a fiber found in everything around them.

But the bay was in danger. The marshes and wildlife too. Cement pilings, broken green glass bottles, and steel cables encroached upon natural living spaces and displaced the animals and the growing grasses. The bay was sick, especially her oysters. The mad harvests depleted the safe beds before natural reproduction had a chance to replenish; there was no consideration of future harvests. Each man took as much as he could get day in and day out. As much as it suffered, the Chincoteague Bay would always outlast the cement pilings and the oil spills.

Of all things living, she would not die.

Natural destruction subsided while a manmade disaster approached Franklin City. Judge Franklin, the benefactor and town father, was long dead and would never know the name of his nemesis, Captain John B. Whealton, a noted "jack of all trades" from Chincoteague Island.

For much of Chincoteague's man-made history, the Whealton family has been one of the most prominent and recognizable names on the island. Watermen, statesmen, farmers, and businessmen – the Whealtons have been all of these and more. That young John B. Whealton would become one of the most important men in the island's history should have surprised no one.

He was born in the spring of 1860, and although he received a rather limited education, his ingenuity and creativity made up for what he lacked in book learning. John Whealton took to the ships and seas at an early age. As with the rest of his family, he was incredibly resourceful and a quick learner. He was only in his twenties when he owned a 4-masted schooner, the *James E. Kelsey*. This was incredible, but he was a Whealton.

Captain Jack sailed all over the world, making several trips to the Orient and the exotic Caribbean. There is a local story about Captain Jack that details his persuasive ability. On one trip to South America, Captain Jack stopped at a port town where Christopher Columbus had been jailed. Legend has it that he was allowed to go into the jail and look around, and after some amount of persuading, Captain Jack boarded his ship with a brick from Columbus's jail cell in hand.

In 1896, Captain Jack was sailing in the Gulf of Mexico when disaster struck. The ship wrecked and he was left drifting in the open waters for two days before being rescued. He vowed he'd never sail again, and he didn't. Captain Jack and his family lived all over the east coast, from Virginia to Florida, wherever his most current endeavor took them. Wherever he was, he was always moving and thinking, building and creating.

But there was always one project that weighed constantly on Captain Jack's mind and he knew he could make it happen. In the 1918, he took his family back to Chincoteague. It was time.

In 1919, Captain Jack organized the Chincoteague Toll Road and Bridge Company. His idea was wild, but nothing short of brilliant. He proposed to build a causeway: a toll road with a series of seven bridges that would connect the island with the mainland of Virginia. During his travels in his younger days, he had seen one of these causeways down in the Florida Keyes. He had long dreamed of doing this for Chincoteague, and once he was back on his home soil,

Captain Jack was able to sell his idea. Automobiles were gaining in popularity as a primary source of transportation. Eastern shore farmers and watermen were seeing possibilities in automobile transportation, especially trucking. They saw trucking as a faster and more direct means of shipping their goods to specific destinations. The islanders backed him and the Virginia General Assembly granted, in September of 1919, the Chincoteague Toll Road and Bridge Company permission to build the causeway. Captain Jack's dream was set into motion.

But the townspeople of Franklin City looked with worry upon the causeway. If the ferries were no longer needed to take people, cars, and goods back and forth to Chincoteague Island, then Franklin City would cease to be important. As a port, it would be rendered useless if the people of Chincoteague no longer needed to use it as a terminus, as a doorway to the rest of the world. As Captain Jack was putting the finishing touches on his new causeway in 1923, the ferries and Franklin City were beginning to look outdated.

The grand opening of the causeway was November 15, 1923. More than 4,000 visitors crowded the small island. Most of the travelers came by way of Captain Jack's famous highway over the bay and though the marshes despite the unpaved state of those marsh roads. The governors of Maryland and Virginia were present at the dedication along with the builders, the Board of Directors of the Chincoteague Toll Road and Bridge Company, but topping that list was the captain himself.

Before the dedication ceremony was over, the sky darkened and rain began to fall on the spectators. As people ran for cover and started home, the sky let loose ripping torrents of rain, which caused the unpaved roads to turn into slipping and sliding mud. Cars and trucks were stuck wheel deep in the marsh muck. The dirt road nearest to the mainland gave way, and it was the last piece to go. By twilight, the proudest day of the island and the doomsday of Franklin City had turned upside down. Ninety-six cars were stuck along seven miles of bridge and mire. For Chincoteague, it was an embarrassment; for the wasting boomtown, it was the final stand.

Captain Jack led the charge to save the visitors; after all, glory and disaster would be attributed to him.

The tourists were rescued from their cars and safely returned to hotels and homes on the island. They waited for the weather to clear and for nature to firm up the marsh patches.

When the sun finally broke the dismal sky, ferries were dispatched to Chincoteague Island to move the cars and people back to Franklin City. From there the visitors gladly welcomed the hard mainland and drove back to their homes, far from the shores of the Chincoteague Bay. The procession of mud covered cars and exhausted people continued for a full two days.

That was the last time cars came across the bay on ferries to Franklin City. The last stand was over and desolation was a vulture circling over the town. Despite its poor beginning, the causeway was the link to independence for the islanders. Captain Jack, his efforts, and his wild idea were celebrated because life, as the island knew it, was changed forever.

For the people of Franklin City, a way of life had passed away.

Despite the losses suffered by the causeway, the town of Franklin City continued on. It was a different sort of existence, much different than the hustle and bustle it was accustomed to. Oysters were still harvested; the trains still ran; and residents still maintained households and small businesses. Willard Dryden continued to sell beef, hams, and chops from his horse-drawn bonnet carriage. The ladies' store, owned by Mrs. Hill, continued to sell garments for the towns' women. The hotel remained busy, renting out rooms to traveling salesmen who took kindly to a clean room and a good meal in the hotel's restaurant. Mr. Gladden, the proprietor of one of Franklin City's general stores, continually offered his patrons more and more amenities, ranging from medicine to meats to shoes. Over at Mr. Coulbourne's store, a waterman could buy parts for his boat while his wife purchased a few groceries. Children could buy drinks from his fastidiously clean soda fountain.

People continued on, living each day from the water and among a subtly changing landscape. Yet the monotony of the town was tragically interrupted by the worst storm to ever hit the eastern shores of Maryland and Virginia.

The skies darkened on August 22, 1933 and many older folks knew instinctively that this storm would not be typical. The Great Storm of 1933 came with a fury that no one had ever seen before or that many would see again. The winds picked up across the bay and burst into Franklin City. Townspeople watched from their windows as the sky swirled above them, forming a menacing tableau of greens, purples, blues and blacks. One of those sets of wide disbelieving eyes belonged to a young girl named Mabel Taylor.

The Taylor family lived in a modest three-story home on Shell Road in Franklin City. Her parents were hand-labelers at the canning factory on the docks of the bay, but like most men in Franklin City, her father also made a living in the fall and winter harvesting oysters. From the living room, the Taylors peered through thin-panned windows, horrified as they watched the sky roll and tumble towards them. There was nowhere to run and fear sank deep into their stomachs. All they could do was watch as the sky tore them apart.

As the storm stalked closer, the ocean flooded the bay. The tides, pushed by the high circling winds, surged up onto the mainland and invaded the empty streets of Franklin City. Lightning struck near the Taylor home and the rain fell harder and harder with each passing moment. Howling winds ripped the shutters off of the home.

"Everybody, get upstairs now!" Charlie Taylor ordered his family. "If you can, grab something and take it with you!"

Her mother and brothers and sisters ran to the stairwell while her father hurried to the front door. "Dear Lord," she heard him say under his breath. "I don't believe this is happening."

Mabel had never heard her father's voice seem so small and uncertain. She turned towards the window and saw waves racing down the street. Frightened, Mabel ran to her father's side. He was pulling a dresser in front of the door in a feeble attempt to bolster the door. Still the ocean water pushed inside from under the doorway. The Chincoteague's waters slithered around their ankles.

"Poppa, what're we gonna..."

She was interrupted by her mother's panicked voice. "Mabel, Charlie, get up here now!"

Mabel saw her father's face was yellow with fear. His large strong shoulders were rounded forward as though the weight upon them was growing heavier by the second. He stood rooted in the muddy water at their feet.

"Poppa, let's go now. Please!" She grabbed at his hand.

He looked down at her. She was right; he couldn't stop the storm from taking his house or dragging it beneath the sea. He couldn't stop the storm from ripping his family away from him. There was no stopping it.

"We best get on upstairs," he told Mabel. "There's nothing we can do now."

Mabel grabbed a little chair that was her sister's and ran as quickly as she possibly could to the third floor. Charlie followed behind her with another chair.

While the storm raged on, Mabel watched out the windows of the third floor attic as furniture from the homes of her neighbors was swept out with the tides. They watched in terror as the flood swallowed a neighbor's home and sucked it beneath the surface of the dark water. Tides surged in and pulled everything of Franklin City back into the sea.

Over her shoulder, Mabel heard the sound of lapping water close by and she turned toward the stairwell. The tide had forced itself all the way up the stairs: the first two floors of their home were completely flooded. The entire family stared at the open pool of water, understanding instantly what it meant. There was no place left to go. No one spoke. The dark water swirled and gurgled, and like a mad dog, it kept them frozen there on the third floor.

Mabel walked toward the stairwell and cautiously peered into the darkness. Her reflection was broken. Other siblings gathered around Mabel's feet and before they could dip their fingers in the water, they were pulled back into the middle of the room by their parents.

"Don't you go anywhere near that stairwell, you hear me?"

Mabel started, "But I..."

"But I nothing! You fall in that water and you'll be swept out clear to Chincoteague! Now stay away from it." She could not disobey the seriousness in her mother's eyes.

"Yes, ma'am."

Mabel took up her seat by the window, while daring to cast furtive glances at the dark pool that kept them prisoners in their attic. Her father sat in a wooden rocker in a far corner, just rocking back and forth with his eyes drawn shut and his thin mouth pursed. Mabel half-imagined him dead.

The storm destroyed their entire town. Streets were flooded two stories deep. The great storm snatched the homes from the land and sacrificed them to the ocean. Guys Point, a barrier island just off the shore, was completely drowned in the awfulness of the storm.

When the Taylors finally came down from the third floor, the putrid smell of earthy marsh assaulted their nostrils. Everything in the home was destroyed – mud caked the walls and floors and stained the ceilings the color of fresh tea. When they made their way out into the street, they saw the canning factory had been completely leveled by the storm. The factory was moved inland. Tomato peels would not stain the marshes again. Many other businesses destroyed by the storm were never rebuilt.

Mabel learned a few days later that the Great Storm had cut an inlet straight through the island community known as Ocean City, completely severing the island in two. Ocean City residents discovered that the storm left a gaping hole in their railroad tracks and had stranded several people whose homes lie on the far side of the new inlet.

The bay visited the Taylor family again three months after the Great Storm. One night in November, Charlie Taylor awoke in the middle of the night, shaking and drenched in sweat. He had had a nightmare.

"Charlie, what's wrong? What's the matter?" His wife looked nearly as panicked as he did.

"I...I had a dream I fell off my boat, and into the water. I tried to fight my way back up, swimming and all, but I kept on getting pulled under. The boat kept drifting farther away from me. My God, I thought I was drowning."

She wrapped her arms around her husband, "It was just a dream. It's ok now." After a few minutes, they fell asleep just inches from one another.

The following day was unseasonably warm for November. Charlie Taylor kissed his wife and boarded his boat to go oystering. The dream still haunted him, but he had told his wife and himself there was nothing to it. "Besides," he told her. "Look at the bay. The water ain't never been that calm. I'll bring you back a whole mess of oysters for supper. Promise."

Mabel was walking home from school that same afternoon when Mrs. McCleary stepped out of her front door. Her stern gray eyes matched the striped apron around her waist.

"Hi, Mrs. McCleary."

"Mabel, you better hurry home. They say your poppa's drowned!" And with that she turned and walked in the house. The door shut heavily behind her.

She ran all the way home, and as she burst through the front door, the faces of her family and close friends told her Mrs. McCleary's awful news was true. Her poppa was gone.

Several watermen had found his boat circling in the Chincoteague Bay and Charlie Taylor was nowhere in sight.

Mabel Taylor was just 13 the year of the Great Storm and her father's death. Thirteen months later, a waterman tonging for oysters in the cold bay found Charlie Taylor standing up on the bottom of the bay. Mabel's mother identified him by his pocket watch.

Franklin City was taking hard, crippling shots. First, the causeway created a decline in business; then came the Great Storm that all but leveled the entire town. All of this on top of a national depression. Not many businessmen wanted to take the risk again because Franklin City just wasn't the town it once was.

As in most other small American towns, the church was always the backbone of Franklin City. The Methodist Episcopal Church, founded on the marshes in 1885, supported the townspeople through the fire of 1896, the floods, the years of oyster population decline, the Great Depression, the lasting effects of the causeway, and the Great Storm of '33 – every birth, death, and marriage too. The residents were so scared by the first fire that they moved the church, in 1898, to a different location away from the train tracks and clustered lots. Methodist Episcopalians came from all over to worship there by the bay.

On Thursday, February 20, 1941, the church erupted in flames. Frantic residents ran from their homes only to stand dumbfounded in the streets, staring at the church. They knew that help would not come quickly enough to save the building so they just watched as their church burned to the ground.

The cause of the fire was later discovered. A resident burning marsh grasses adjacent to the church lost control of the fire. Embers, the man said, just leapt onto the church's wooden siding and burrowed a smoking hole. For a second, no damage was noticeable. Then smoke steadily arose from the side of the church and then flames began to kick out the wooden paneling. The responsible resident ran to phone for the fire department in Stockton, Maryland. Pocomoke City and Chincoteague Island fire departments also responded to the scene, but their collective efforts were in vain. The church was a total loss.

George Hearthway, the lay leader, was the most devastated of all the onlookers. Next to the minister, he was the very pulse of the church. Members often joked that he was the stone on which the church in Franklin City was built. George Hearthway stood in front of the ashes of his church, and deep in his chest, he knew it was over.

Members of the congregation rushed to Franklin City when they heard the tragic news. Mae and Ed Tarr, a young married couple from Girdletree, Maryland who attended the church regularly, were among the first visitors. Mae gripped her husband's arm as they neared the terrible scene. The smoldering remains of the pews lay like charred casualties, exposed and horrific. The altar was scorched and cracked. No one wanted to see it, but everyone stared with eyes unblinking, mouths agape. Mae allowed her eyes to wander, and something strange caught her attention in the marsh behind the church. The leaves of burned bibles were spread out over the marsh like ten thousand burned butterflies.

Mae stared at the ashes. That the church was gone seemed like a violation of everything that was right. God was homeless in Franklin City.

George Hearthway consoled the congregation and gave them the worst of the news. The church was not going to be rebuilt. He told them that they would be joining the Methodist Protestant Church in Greenbackville. George worked hard to get them separate services until the final preparations for the full integration of the two congregations could be made. The Franklin City church members looked up to George Hearthway because he was, as the locals said, a good man, and they could trust him as he led them down the road to Greenbackville.

But for the strong, surviving people of Franklin City, this final blow broke their backs. What was the use, they wondered, of continually rebuilding a town that seemed destined to die right there on the water's edge? They left the church in a heap of ashes and passed it each Sunday on their way to services in Greenbackville.

Without a church and the plentitude of oysters, Franklin City slumped into slow decay. Businesses began leaving and residents sold their homes for more stable and prosperous places. With fewer people and businesses, the trains stopped running. In the early 1940s, the last train left Franklin City and did not return; a few years later, the last working business – a restaurant – left the failed boomtown. From that moment, Franklin City had been abandoned.

But not all life was gone.

In the late 1950s, the local teenagers from Greenbackville would steal away on Friday and Saturday nights and sneak into the old Redmen's lodge in Franklin City. With a record player blaring Elvis, they would rock the very foundation of the building that in a previous life had been a general store. Young boys took recess on the large front porch to unwind cigarette packs from their sleeves and have a cool time smoking and keeping the girls waiting. But the girls never minded their absence because the boys always came back. Someone always brought Coca-Colas; somebody always stole cookies and sweets from their mother's cupboards. Record after record, dance after dance, and kiss after kiss, until the teenagers had to go, old Franklin City almost lived again.

Other than the juke joint days of the late 1950s, many of the buildings simply stood as dilapidated reminders of something that had once been and never would be again. They stood empty and they rotted for years.

With one final act of attrition, a powerful storm demolished the ghost town in 1962. The great storm slammed into the Atlantic coastline with such ferocity and aggression that record tides were simply obliterated. Entire buildings just vanished beneath the magnetic tides of the Atlantic Ocean. Once again, the tides ripped at the land, pulling anything it could into the dark waters.

When the storm left, less than half of Franklin City's land remained and only six houses and the old Redman's lodge were left standing. The dream of Judge Franklin was as dead as he was and his mistakes had been washed out to sea and washed clean of all that remained. Finally, there was peace on the Chincoteague Bay as the name of the place was slowly forgotten and, as one by one, its former residents moved away or died.

At the end of Swan Gut Road in Accomack County, Virginia, there is a sharp right turn. Follow that road for a while, being mindful of the curves, and soon the dead buildings and tall reeds will form a strange tunnel to the Chincoteague Bay. The road is narrow, rounded with age; there is only one road now, and it stops just a few feet short of a shoreline of oyster shells and small, rolling waves.

Perched among the salty reeds and marshes that have regenerated themselves over the last two generations, Franklin City slowly vanishes away. It decays a little more each day and immeasurably with each storm. No zip code is known, no dot on a map proves its modern day existence, and the inhabitants have slipped away or passed on. The only communication in the ghost town is the waves that ebb and flow between its deserted shores and Chincoteague Island. Once hailed as one of the largest ports of its kind, Franklin City is now the most uninhabited place of secrets on the Eastern Shore.

Across the bay, Chincoteague Island thrives with a newfound source of income – tourism. As it turned out, the wild ponies of the island captivated the nation's heart when Margaret Henry's book, <u>Misty of Chincoteague</u>, became an award winning best-seller. Even today, people come from all over the country each year to Chincoteague Island, especially during the famous pony swim and Pony Penning. They can't help wanting to buy a little piece of Chincoteague.

Chincoteague Island and its people continue on. Few people even know that Franklin City ever existed, and the few who remember are slipping away.

Mabel Taylor became Mabel Jones four years after that awful year of 1933. She and Garland Jones, her husband of more than 60 years, have both passed. They lived for years in a modest home in a town called Girdletree, just a few miles from what was Franklin City.

The home Mabel was raised in has been rotting beneath the Chincoteague Bay for decades. As she grew into her silver years, she watched as the bustling town she knew as a child became an empty shell. I often wonder if she ever suspected that something was wrong in Franklin City.

I have traveled the length of the marshes and her roads. A short distance away from Franklin City is the Union Franklin City Cemetery. It is a small graveyard filled with old dates and worn names on moss and lichen covered monuments to the dead. The graves give a silent roll call: Hudsons, Hancocks, Howards, Taylors, Crowleys, fallen soldiers, a young firefighter, husbands and wives, small children and newborns, and a few souls left unmarked. Charlie Taylor is buried there. So is George Hearthway.

But there is a telling inscription on the grave of a man named Samuel J. Crowley. He was born in 1841 and died in 1921. He would have known Franklin City in a way that no one today can imagine. His tombstone reads: *"Pleased are the dead which die in the Lord. Gone but not forgotten."*

I cannot say what moves a person to shudder when a gull cries on the Chincoteague Bay nor do I know why I continually feel the steady pressure of unseen eyes when I face the water with the reeds at my back. No one lives there now, but something keeps Franklin City breathing, alive underneath the dead shells of oysters and buildings.

When the sun sets, I am always leaving.

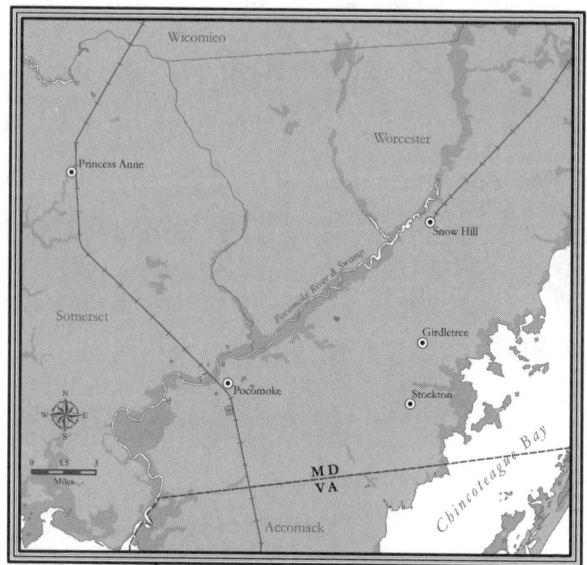

Lower Eastern Shore, Maryland

AND JUSTICE FOR ALL

Briar patches laced in ice framed a sky that grew steadily darker. They gripped their guns firmly with purpose and slipped through the backwoods. An old hound followed closely behind the two men. Just as quickly as the sun had set on that blistering cold day, they moved upon the Pilchard's farmhouse. Winter air bit at their faces, yet they remained undeterred from their mission. There was a plan.

They passed M.P. Selby's sawmill, which was the closest piece of property to the Pilchard farm. It stood cold and unlit. Snow muffled their heavy steps as they advanced on towards the white and green two-story home. Moving as silently as they could along the side of the house, they took a turn for the back porch where they slit a segment of mesh screen and removed it.

The Pilchards were home. There would be no turning back now.

The winter of 1940 buried the people of the Delmarva Peninsula as blizzards raged on for days, freezing nearly everything in sight. The small towns of the Eastern Shore of Maryland and the Eastern Shore of Virginia were paralyzed in the early days of February. People were barricaded indoors for weeks, listening to their radios for any signs of relief. Everyone was waiting for the cold to break and for a moment of better news, something other than Hitler's latest maneuverings.

The aging couple had been snowed in for weeks and had only gained access to the county's small highway a few days prior. Finally, the snow was beginning to melt away. Inside the large house, partly camouflaged by the snow, the living room was bright and delicately framed in a yellow glow. A familiar program was playing on the dual-knobbed radio, a little static resonated through the room; otherwise, it was fine entertainment for the old couple. Harvey Pilchard was relaxing while his wife, Annie, wrote a letter to their daughter who lived in Wilmington, Delaware. It was Sunday, February 11, 1940.

"My Dear Daughter," she wrote. "Your father and I are sitting here thinking of you. We have been to church twice today (Sunday), and have just listened to our favorite radio program." She marked a time of 8:10 p.m. above her daughter's Wilmington address and continued the letter onto a second page.

Harvey bent forward in his chair and looked towards the kitchen. He had heard a strange noise and left his warm chair to go investigate.

Annie's letter abruptly ended as a shotgun blast ripped through her husband.

She jumped from her chair and saw Harvey stagger backwards into the kitchen, and then into the living room. Annie screamed. He looked at his wife with one hand over his stomach: "I've been shot."

Blood stained his shirt and streamed through his fingers. Before Annie had a chance to reach her husband, two men burst into the room, one with a shotgun and the other with a revolver. She caught a glimpse of her husband's body hitting the floor. The men moved upon her. "Get your money or we'll kill you."

Annie started into the front stairway – her purse was in a bureau drawer in her bedroom on the second floor. The men scuffed their heavy hip boots on the floor as they pushed her towards the stairwell. The barrel of a gun nudged Annie along.

Before her foot touched the first step, the cold barrel slid down the small of her back. One of the men grabbed a fistful of her graying hair and Annie's thick neck stiffly arched. The man spun her around and knocked her hard to the floor. Laying the shotgun to one side, he stood over her body. He had already calculated his second revenge. The other man stepped aside and moved back. He just watched.

Annie desperately tried to regain her footing, but he pulled her to him, away from the stairs. She searched his dark face as he bent close to her – there was something about him. She raced through the catalogue of people in her mind, and at last, Annie Pilchard realized that she knew exactly who he was. He snatched her up by the fat of her underarms, his dirty fingernails cutting through her faded housecoat.

Annie pleaded. Begged. Promised anything, everything. She cried.

"Don't you move an' I'll let you go." He pushed his body onto hers.

He knew she recognized him – he saw the flash in her eyes. It had only been three years since she last saw him. Her body twisted beneath him and her eyes grew large. His breath snaked into her ears and slithered down the side of her exposed neck. Annie fought back, but her age and sex didn't help her. The man pushed his hands between her housecoat and her body, dragging his callused fingers along her skin. His sweat dripped into the deep lines around her mouth. The intention was absolutely clear. There was a sharp searing pain, and then she felt her mind disconnect.

While she was pinned to the hallway floor, her husband lay only feet from her. The second man stood deep in the shadows of the hallway and said nothing.

The radio echoed softly from the nearby living room. The letter to her daughter was unfinished. He raped her in the house in which she had raised her child, in the house that she had shared with the only man she ever loved. *He raped her in her home.* She looked in the direction of the living room with bleary eyes: Harvey Pilchard was dead now.

Just as quickly as it began, it was over. The man clumsily slipped off her round body, and pulled himself to his feet, fixing his trousers as he stood. He took a few slow steps away from her as though to survey the damage. Annie Pilchard, with her head turned away from the men, slowly reached her hands to her waist to pull her housecoat back down.

"Come on, we ain't here for this. We're here for the money." The man in the shadows finally spoke.

They moved towards her. Annie said nothing. She moved nothing.

The man she knew snatched her up by the arms again, and pulled her wet face close to his. "Where's your money?"

"Upstairs, in my purse."

"That's a good girl." His eyes were like a nightmare that she couldn't pull away from.

The man in the shadows stepped forward and they pulled her to her feet. She staggered and they pushed her, forcing her up the stairwell. Once upstairs, Annie took her purse from the bedroom bureau and gave them everything the purse held – eighteen dollars in scattered change.

The coins and bills were quickly summed in their hands and their faces turned downward. The eighteen dollars was not enough, although it would go far for a couple of poor farmhands. The Pilchards had money and they knew it. They had dreamed of small piles of bills and jars full of coins; they had planned to take all of it with them. But this night had not gone as planned.

"Get all your money!"

"That's it. That's all I've left!" She took a step back and turned away from them. All was confusion. She stared at her bed, the one she had made that morning after Harvey finally rose. "Time for church," she remembered saying to him.

The men were whispering to each other. Annie's feet rooted themselves into the floor.

"Time to go, Harvey," she had called to him just that morning. Her mind was a tangle of old memories and horrible new ones.

They no longer whispered. She heard the clicking of a metal hammer. Nothing could change this room back to what it was, she thought, as a bullet slammed into her back, ripping through layers of fat and muscle accumulated through years of being a farmer's wife.

Annie Pilchard's body hit the bedroom floor, and the men, believing her dead, continued the search for more money downstairs.

Her eyes fluttered open and the haze of disorientation settled around her. She struggled for a brief second. Then she remembered.

Oh God, she remembered.

Seriously wounded, but far from dead, Annie raised herself and grabbed a small, white blanket from the bed just within her reach. As she wrapped it around herself, she distinctly heard their voices and footsteps downstairs. Her chest felt heavy as though the bullet inside weighed a thousand pounds. She tried to pull herself together. One thought pushed her to action – what if they came back upstairs?

Annie dragged herself across the room and crawled out a bedroom window onto a small ledge over the back porch. From her hiding spot on top of the porch, she could hear them talking. Annie saw them leave the house and walk out into the yard. One of the men wanted to leave – the other wanted to stay and keep searching. She was afraid, more afraid than she had ever been in her life. Fearing that she might be seen, she went back inside the bedroom. Annie needed a better place to hide. But where? Her mind reeled and she knew she didn't have time to think. Where? She looked around, searching, and then she knew – the attic.

Once back inside the bedroom, she slipped off her shoes to ensure that she wouldn't be too loud and pulled the quilt from the bed for warmth. Her housecoat clung cold and wet to her back. The attic was accessible and it was her only option. Pausing for a moment, she realized they were coming back into the house.

While the men ransacked the lower portion of the house searching for stashed money and valuables, Annie crawled on her hands and knees through the musty maze of boxes and old furniture, dead bugs and a lifetime of forgotten things. She headed for a dormer window on the front side of the house. As she shifted her weight like a large cat, blood rivulets trickled down her fleshy sides. Shallow breaths allowed her to hear the men destroying her home. She imagined them throwing furniture and emptying neatly arranged drawers, scattering papers and pictures, and stepping over Harvey's dead body. The pain in her chest reminded her the nightmare was real and the voices downstairs reminded her that it wasn't over.

Slowly and quietly, Annie raised the dormer window. The window was small, but she managed to thread herself through the wooden frame. After squeezing her body through the opening, Annie snuck out onto the small roof ledge. She pulled herself up onto the roof of the house, and found a hiding place behind the front chimney and inside of a roof crevice. She hid down in that spot and wrapped the quilt around her.

Annie knew, at least for a moment, she was safe.

The search had been unsuccessful. The Pilchards money and valuables must have been well hidden because they couldn't find a single hiding spot. The money, they decided, must be stashed away in the bedroom, and they could tear that room apart easily.

They came back to the bedroom and panic stopped them in the doorway. Mrs. Pilchard was gone!

The raid had taken a sharp turn for the worst – they had gained only a small amount of the anticipated money and a witness to their crimes. They knew she could identify one of them to the authorities and she was their problem now. The money seemed almost insignificant.

As they tore apart the bedroom, they knew if they didn't find her and kill her, then she would talk.

"She's around here somewhere!"

When they were satisfied that she wasn't in the bedroom any longer, they ran downstairs and out into the yard.

From her vantage point on the roof, she watched them search for her. Now the men had flashlights and she could see the lights shining all around the yard, outbuildings, and into the house. Not even the old hound could help them pick up a trace of her. As quietly as she could, Annie pulled the quilt tight around her injured body and eased her back against the icy bricks of the chimney. She wondered how bad the gunshot wound was. She wondered if she would die right there on the roof of her house.

With the hound on their heels, the two men ran into the woods, flashing their lights all around them. Perhaps she had escaped from the house and was hiding in the woods, but wherever she was, Mrs. Pilchard was not inside that bedroom where her fat body dropped to the floor. They never intended to leave them alive. The plan had been so simple: slip in, a couple of shots, get the money, and slip out. The Pilchards were rich, they knew it, and the money was supposed to be stashed in thick wads in the drawers and stuck inside coffee pots. It was supposed to have been easy.

Annie Pilchard was the worst complication.

She lay wide-awake, straining her ears for any sound. Her husband of more than thirty years was dead; she remembered his face when he hit the living room floor. As soon as she recalled one memory, a hundred more flooded in to take its place. She remembered his deep voice, that low singing voice he saved for church.

During service that morning, he sang especially loud and smiled down into her face. He was happy just to be out of the house. His quiet singing looks reminded her of the way he did everything – slowly and precisely. As her check brushed the coarse brick of chimney wall, she was reminded of the cold and the wetness and the ache in her chest. Harvey was gone. She had been violated, shot, and left for dead. In the space of mere minutes, her life took on an empty, alien shape. It was now a foreign form without purpose. Her private thoughts were interrupted: the men had come back from the woods.

Annie held her breath.

The flashlights bounced wildly off the snow-covered buildings and nearby trees. They talked in the yard as they searched. As they got closer to the house, their words echoed through the winter night: "We've got to kill her before she talks!" The lights disappeared and she strained her ears for any sounds. She knew instinctively that they were desperate to find her.

Annie lay silent on the cold rooftop, afraid that the slightest sound might give her away, while the men continued to search and destroy. After a short time, the two men abandoned their search and escaped into the woods. They did not return.

All she could do was wait for dawn.

John T. Manuel was on his way to work at M.P. Selby's sawmill. A distinct sound caught his ear; something strange and slightly removed, like an animal pinned in a trap. Moving towards the direction of the sound, he realized it was a woman screaming. But where could she be? The nearest property was the Pilchard farm. The screams got louder as he approached the house.

He called out, not knowing where the woman might be. Annie answered his call. She told him to go for help, told him that she had been shot. John Manuel turned his disbelieving eyes towards the roof – Mrs. Pilchard was on top of her house!

Immediately, John Manuel alerted the Stockton Volunteer Fire Department that there was a serious emergency on Stockton Road at the Pilchard farm. The fire department rushed to the scene where they were met by police officers, Sheriff William Hall and a young country lawyer named William G. Kerbin, Jr. from Snow Hill, Maryland.

Someone else ran for a doctor.

Once the firemen had safely returned Annie Pilchard to the ground, the local physician examined Annie, especially the dangerous position of the gunshot wound in her back. She was rushed to Peninsula General Hospital in Salisbury, Maryland. From her hospital room, Annie Pilchard recounted the night to the officers and William Kerbin.

In 1937, Harvey Pilchard testified against one of his farmhands, Arthur Collick. The 25-year old Negro, accused of stealing chickens from the farm, was charged with theft and sentenced to three years in the Maryland State Penitentiary. Three months after Arthur Collick's release, Harvey Pilchard was dead.

This is the man Annie named.

Just before dawn, just hours before Annie was found on her roof, Arthur Collick started running. If Annie Pilchard survived the night, then it was only a matter of time before the police came for him. He had to leave, but his family could not stay behind. Martha

Blake, his common-law wife, and Virginia Lillian, her daughter, knew why there was blood on his hands. He knew he had no choice but to take the Blake women with him. Before the sun put the day's events in motion, Arthur Collick and the Blakes started running, scared and directionless.

Martha Blake had waited three years for her Arthur to get out of prison and come back home. She and her daughter maintained the little house outside of Girdletree, a little town about four miles north of Stockton. When he finally returned, he was not the same man. The three years in the Maryland State Penitentiary hardened the youthful roundness of his face into coarse slabs of thick skin, and his eyes, permanently watchful, no longer danced when she came in the front door. For three months, they lived like strangers and then, one cold night in February, it was over.

Martha and her daughter were now homeless and at the mercy of a man she loved but no longer knew. Arthur Collick took them from shelter and led them into the unforgiving terrain of Worcester County backwoods in the middle of the coldest month in years. No shelter, no food, and no water; survival was not only a preoccupation, it was doubtful.

When dusk fell on Monday night, they were desperate for aid. The Blake women turned to Arthur for guidance. Temperatures were slightly above freezing and each of them was poorly dressed. Night fell too quickly.

He led them to the home of Weldon Ewell, a black sharecropper on the Preston Bounds farm. All three stood barefoot in front of his cabin. Collick beat on the door, "Weldon! Weldon, we need help!"

Weldon Ewell came to the door and recognized Arthur Collick and his women. He already received word of the Pilchard man's death, and he knew that every white man in a 30-mile radius wanted Collick and anyone associated with him.

"I can't help you. Now, get away from here!" He feared Arthur Collick for one reason only – guilt by association.

The Blakes pleaded with him, and Weldon almost wanted to help the crying women, seeing their barefoot, poorly dressed figures shivering on his porch. The air was slightly above freezing, and Weldon Ewell almost froze just looking at them. Martha's eyes were large and dark, like the eyes of a fallen doe.

"Please, Weldon, you got to help us." Collick begged. Ewell could not afford to risk his place on the white farm for three wanted fugitives.

"I said it before, I can't help you. Now get on!" He turned his face from the sadness – he couldn't look at them – and slammed the wooden door. They listened as the bolt slid into place, and they realized that he would not be the last to turn them away and that his door would not be the last to shut them out. Collick pulled the two women to him and he hurried them off the porch. The young Blake girl dragged her feet and her sobs echoed back to Weldon, who watched from his window.

Giving them enough time to make it into the woods and get far enough away, he reported his contact with Arthur Collick and the Blakes to the authorities. Weldon Ewell had done all he could do.

Arthur Collick still had some of Pilchard's money, and he formulated a new plan. Since the Blakes were not as easy to identify, he would send one of them to call on Pettigrew Bunn, the manager of the E. James

Reid general store in Welbourne, a town just southwest of Stockton. Running with empty stomachs was making them weak and to survive the night, they needed as much strength as they could muster.

Around 9:30 p.m., Martha Blake beat on the door of Pettigrew Bunn's home. She told Bunn that she wanted to buy food from the general store – she and her infant baby had run out of food. Bunn, although suspicious, allowed the woman into the store where she purchased $1.25 worth of food. She thanked him and left, but as she walked down towards the road, Bunn saw two figures emerge from the roadside brush and join her. Just as quickly as they had come, they vanished into the darkness.

Once authorities received word that the possible suspects were asking for aid in the Girdletree vicinity, they immediately dispatched officers to the area. Local men from all over Worcester County grabbed their shotguns and hunting rifles and formed a large posse, vowing vengeance on the head of Arthur Collick and his accomplice. The white community was intoxicated with rage and rumor; the eyes of the black community grew wide and watchful. There were no safe places anymore: the manhunt had begun.

Tuesday morning brought widespread news of the attack in Stockton. Newspapers widely reported the malicious deeds of the "Negro slayers." Annie Pilchard's rape was also made a headline. The doctors reported she was in stable condition, but the bullet was lodged too deep inside her chest cavity to consider removal. The only predicable complication was a possibility of pneumonia from her overnight exposure on the icy roof so she remained hospitalized.

Maryland State Police officers and local authorities worked all Monday setting up the crime scene and preserving what evidence was left behind. A row of two by fours lined a path marking footprints near the side and back of the house. The slit screen on the porch was marked in a big X with white tape and an officer recovered a bullet from the front stairway. Fingerprint experts were ordered to the scene to canvas the house while detectives examined bloodstains in the bedroom. All this to build a case that Annie Pilchard alone could deliver.

Cars lined both sides of Stockton Road as well as nearby lanes. More than a hundred people came from miles around just to stand in front of the house and mill around the perimeter of the property. Nothing was left at the house but every person in the county wanted to be a part of the small town scandal. The entire area was crawling with curious locals while only a few miles away, Arthur Collick and the two women had sought refuge in Dunn Swamp, parts of which were still frozen from the last blizzard.

The search for the murder suspect and the Blake women was the topic of conversation around crossroads stores and gas stations throughout Worcester and the surrounding counties. The newest rumor or bit of information was like a pinch of adrenaline or a shot of alcohol, producing a heady rush of emotion and nervous energy. Men sat around pot-bellied stoves in general stores fantasizing about catching the already infamous Arthur Collick. Women kept their children inside and their gossip circling.

PHOTOGRAPH APPEARED IN THE DEMOCRATIC MESSENGER ON FEBRUARY 15, 1940

CAPTION READS: "Arrow points to roof of her home, where Mrs. Pilchard, shot in back, crawled from attic window to top of house behind chimney shown in photo, to escape two negro slayers. She remained hidden on the roof all Sunday night for over ten hours, before daylight brought help Monday."

PHOTOGRAPH APPEARED IN THE DEMOCRATIC MESSENGER ON FEBRUARY 15, 1940.

CAPTION READS: "Among the first Worcester County officers to reach the Pilchard farm home Monday morning were Sheriff J. William Hall, of Berlin; Deputy Sheriff Harry C. Bradford and Deputy Sheriff W. Rhodes Rew, of Snow Hill. Deputy Rew is also Police Chief in Snow Hill."

PHOTOGRAPH APPEARED IN THE DEMOCRATIC MESSENGER ON FEBRUARY 15, 1940

CAPTION READS: "These two negro women, Martha Blake, 31(left) and her daughter, Lillian, 14, are being held for questioning in the slaying Sunday night of Harvey Pilchard, Stockton, Md., farmer. This photo was taken shortly after their arrest early Tuesday by Sheriff J. William Hall (left) and Pocomoke Police Chief A. W. Brittingham. There were supposed to be able to give information concerning the main culprit, Collick, but he is still at large, and is supposed either to have escaped or perished from exposure in the swamp where he was hiding."

PHOTOGRAPH OF MARTHA (LEFT) AND VIRGINIA LILLIAN BLAKE (RIGHT) APPEARED IN THE WORCESTER DEMOCRAT ON FEBRUARY 19, 1940.

PHOTOGRAPH OF ARTHUR COLLICK APPEARED IN THE SALISBURY TIMES ON JULY 30, 1940.

Three local men – Buck Sharpley, Joe Hill, and Fred Hill – were patrolling a road that lead to Virginia and passed by the swamp. The authorities had not deputized any of the men; the citizens took it upon themselves to help out. As the three men made their way down the road, Arthur Collick, Martha Blake, and Virginia Blake stepped out of the woods about fifty yards in front of them. Fred Hill raised his rifle and fired into the air to scare them.

The women stopped in the road, but Arthur Collick turned for the woods and started to run. Quickly, Joe Hill raised his rifle and shot directly at Collick. The men ran to the spot where Collick bolted into the woods, but he was gone. The shot was not fatal.

They captured the barefoot women and took them into Pocomoke City.

Arthur Collick was entirely alone in the swamp now, only this time he was injured. The posse man's shot damaged his right hand. Doing his best to nurse his bloody hand, Arthur continued to search for a hiding place deep in the swamp. He kept moving, thick briars ripping at his arms and legs. Large, dark trees provided him with camouflage from the planes overhead. The cypress swamp was alive. It crawled with people looking as hard for him as he was a place to rest.

A posse of over five hundred men – none of whom were deputized – scoured the cypress swamp with rifles and shotguns. The Maryland State Police turned their three best bloodhounds loose in the swamp, but the dogs were unable to detect a scent. Too many men stalked the swamp.

His situation was already getting worse by the moment. The bloodhounds barked in the distance and the voices of men were heard in between the dogs. Airplanes buzzed low over the treetops like a swarm of honeybees. Everyone in the area was looking for him and he knew survival meant finding food, but staying alive meant staying clear of the posse.

He heard a voice nearby and his heart froze solid in his breathless chest. Three men were walking about a hundred yards from him. He could run, but he'd be shot. He could stand still, but he'd be found. Arthur pressed his back hard into a tree. Maybe if he pushed hard enough, he'd actually become part of the slimy, moss-covered bark. How could he run away without making a sound? How could he become invisible while covered in blood? Someone called out for the men to hurry quickly and the three men took off in the opposite direction, leaving Arthur poised to run.

By the late afternoon of Tuesday, the posse had swelled to number over eight hundred men and there was still no trace of him anywhere. William Kerbin expressed his frustration in the papers: "Our men can almost surround the swamp, but he has some way of getting out we haven't found yet." Had Arthur Collick vanished into the February air like some kind of menacing ghost? Every time he heard the voices and the dogs, he dropped to the ground and pushed himself into the trees, briar patches, dead logs, whatever he could find. This way, he slipped in and out of the posse's grasp.

The Blake women, during questioning, told officers they had been with Arthur Collick since early Monday morning, wandering the woods and fields of Worcester County. They also implicated his accomplice – a young farmhand by the name of Charles Manuel. At 5:00 on Tuesday afternoon, police arrested the teenager at his home in Stockton and took him to the jail in Snow Hill. The Blake women also had been transported to that same jail after their capture in Pocomoke earlier that day. Another man, George Selby, was implicated as a lookout and he was also tracked down and taken to the jail.

With two suspects and Arthur's family in jail and with two hundred more men joining the swelling ranks of the posse, Arthur Collick's chances were slimming down to nothing.

Tension was growing in the thousand-man, independent posse. The men had been dredging tirelessly through the swamp since the early morning, some even from the night before. No man would sleep as long as Arthur Collick was alive and running. Aware of the anxiety growing in the nearby towns, the Maryland State Police split up the suspects at the request of William Kerbin who had gotten wind that a group of men planned to break into the jail and take Charles Manuel. Officers immediately sent Manuel to a jail in Easton, Maryland; George Selby was also moved in case of an attempt. The Blake women, unfortunately, remained in Snow Hill at the Worcester County jail.

Just moments after Manuel's remand to Talbot County, a rumor hit the swamp: Arthur Collick had been captured and taken to Snow Hill. Without hesitation, scores of cars were on the move and headed straight towards the quiet jail town.

A mob quickly gathered outside of the tiny building. Their voices, screaming for Collick, reverberated through the night and into the jail. They heaved and moved as one giant mass, trampling the jail's wooden fence and wielding the broken pieces as weapons.

Inside the jail, tension was mounting. Gerald Bowen, who was the jailer, and four officers tried to ignore the noise while Sheriff William Hall advised the 12 inmates to keep calm. Among those 12 were Martha and Virginia Blake.

There was a pounding on the jail door. Sheriff Hall, with his hand resting on the gun at his side, opened the door.

The mob roared for Collick's release, bellowing with one ugly mouth, "Turn the damn nigger over to us!"

"You've always known me to play fair with you boys," Sheriff Hall faced the crowd. "There's only two women in there."

"You've been bought!" The mob roared again, but Sheriff Hall would not move. They cried and moaned, but the disappointed mob dispersed. After the mob disbanded, Sheriff Hall and the four officers left the small jail, citing a lack of sleep. The jailer was left alone with the prisoners.

Noticing the absence of the sheriff, the mob returned and surrounded the small brick jail. Local men were armed with hacksaws, crowbars, and rope. They sawed an iron crossbar out of a window on the east side of the building. Ropes were then tied to the remaining bars. The men worked as one giant muscle, pulling against the ropes. The more the window cracked, the harder they strained. At last, the frame of the window gave way and broke completely free from the wall. Like animals, the men clawed at the bricks and mortar to make a larger hole. The jailer watched helplessly as the wall crumbled and mob members poured inside.

A white man with a rope rattled the bars of the Blakes' cell. With fat fingers he made a noose and spat as he waved it in front of them: "How'd you like to have this around your neck?"

Martha pushed her daughter into the farthest corner of their cell and covered her with her body. They watched as the men began sawing the locks off each jail cell. Each prisoner was instructed to get away from the building. A white man with sweat rolling down his balding head turned the hacksaw on the lock of the Blakes' cell. Martha and Virginia Lillian did not doubt their impending fate. The lock broke. The jail door was yanked open. Four white men stepped inside.

No time was wasted. The screaming women were dragged from their cell and pushed into cars that sped away towards Stockton.

Martha and Virginia were the only tangible connection the mob had to Arthur Collick – to lynch them would be to lynch their only hopes of catching him. No, there had to be a better way of getting the information out of them. A few mob members decided to buy them off. The Blakes were taken to the R. L. Mason General Store where a few men purchased food, socks, and shoes for them. Now, it was time to talk. The men insisted that the Blakes give up all their information about Arthur Collick. And the women cooperated, but only for a short time.

Four Maryland State Police officers arrived in Stockton only minutes behind the mob. Their orders came directly from Maryland Governor Herbert R. O'Conor: save the witnesses by any means necessary, consider the technicalities afterward. With nightsticks, they muscled their way through the crowd trying to reach the Blake women.

As the officers neared the hostages, several of the mob members grabbed one of the police officers and pushed him to the ground, beating his head and body with fists and sticks. Just as another officer reached out for Martha Blake, a shot ripped passed them.

The policemen surrounded their fallen man, and drew their weapons. The mob backed down for a moment. Although badly beaten, the trooper wasn't gravely injured, and he was helped to his feet. They aimed their guns into the heart of the crowd.

One more shot, they declared, one more move and someone here will die. But neither the mob, the police, nor the hostages knew who that would be.

In a swift movement, two troopers seized the women and, covering their lean bodies with their own, pushed them through the crowd. Suddenly, everyone was moving and another shot sizzled past the officers and the Blake women. The other two officers returned the mob's fire. A bullet pierced through the leg of a man, ripping a quarter-sized hole through the top of his kneecap. The officers shoved the Blakes into police cars and busted loose from the throng of angry white men.

In the center of Pocomoke, the mob had reformed. Police informed the mob the night was over. All four suspects had been taken to the Western Shore for safekeeping. Only Arthur Collick remained at large on the Eastern Shore; the search would reconvene in the morning.

And the mob was finished.

Harvey W. Pilchard was buried on Wednesday – Valentine's Day. More than 500 people turned out to pay their respects. His obituary read: "An enterprising farmer, the deceased was a valued neighbor and a kind husband and father. He was loved by everyone that knew him. He was a member of the Baptist faith." His wife, his daughter, six sisters, and a brother survived Harvey. Annie Pilchard was unable to attend her husband's funeral; she remained under physician's care in a hospital 30 miles away.

Governor O'Conor in Annapolis was not going to take chances with the folks on the lower shore. When he had heard of the troubles, he sent reinforcements, saying that "every necessary step must be taken for the maintenance of law and order." His official report from the police numbered the crowd at 1,000 men. The passion incited by the riots of Tuesday's mobs had subsided and 32 more state police officers flooded the area at the Governor's request.

The governor had serious concerns about the mob's actions. Jail attacks had been attempted and successful. The Eastern Shore was in heated upheaval – only two years prior a mob lynched a black man who was accused of raping a white woman. O'Conor demanded action to prevent further lynchings. The necessity of extra force could not be stressed enough because more than half of the lynchings that occurred in the state happened on the Eastern Shore or on her rural counterpart of Southern Maryland.

Even the regional leaders of the AFL-CIO were concerned about the welfare of Eastern Shore Negroes. The president of the Maryland and District of Columbia Industrial Union Council expressed his fears in a telegram to Governor O'Conor. He asked for State Police protection, stating that he "could not find language strong enough with which to urge you to take every possible precaution against lynching on the Eastern Shore."

"Lynching or even an attempted lynching," he wrote, "is a crime against all of society and would leave an ugly blot upon the state of Maryland."

Officially, or at least in the papers, Sheriff Hall washed his hands of Tuesday night: "There has been no demand for action against the mob," he said. "We have identified at least 40 and perhaps more of the men, and all of them are from other counties. We have no plan of action now. We know the ringleaders of the mob, and feel that the situation is well in hand. I experienced no trouble with our local county boys last night. It's the outsiders that cause trouble like ours last night." There would be no investigation led and no charges pressed against the men who destroyed the Snow Hill jail and kidnapped two state witnesses.

Even William Kerbin, the Worcester County state's attorney, remained tight-lipped about the mob. Leading the investigation, he told the local papers, was not his job. "My only task is to prepare cases against such persons as may be arrested by the Sheriff. We have not heard any complaints from any parties, nor have had any formal charges filed with us." The "parties" included Martha and Virginia Lillian Blake – the kidnapped women who knew so much about Arthur Collick and so little of his whereabouts. Filing a formal complaint was out of their collective reach: two Negro women pressing charges against more than 40 white men was as outlandish and absurd as it was dangerous.

William G. Kerbin Jr. had been recently appointed the State's Attorney for Worcester County, just two years before the events of the Pilchard case became one of the most notorious of all criminal suits in Maryland. William Kerbin was a born and bred Worcester County boy. He received his law degree from the University of Baltimore in 1932 and passed the Bar exam one year later.

The Kerbin family was entrenched in the tradition of law and community. His father had served in the same position that he now held. William G. Kerbin, Jr. was faced with a delicate dance: the slightest misjudgment could cause this case to violently erupt and he was at the center of it.

William Kerbin had been the one to order the removal of witnesses from the Eastern Shore, and since that decision, he had received several death threats against himself and his family. His young wife feared for their safety, and Kerbin wasn't about to chance the passions of the mob. He had seen what they were capable of. Three state troopers took up rooms in the family home and Kerbin carried a loaded .32 pistol on him at all times.

The death threats continued day and night because, as far as the callers were concerned, Kerbin was protecting black men who had killed a white man and attacked a white woman. The community was turning on him and he found himself in extremely unfamiliar and uncomfortable territory.

Kerbin, as the days dragged past, became aware of his critical role in the case. He would be a focal point

– Annie Pilchard, Arthur Collick, and himself. The murder in Worcester County was receiving tri-state attention, and every word that William G. Kerbin, Jr. said was taken down and reported in every town and almost every county in Maryland, Delaware, and Virginia. For the young state's attorney, this case was a monumental moment in his career, provided both Arthur Collick and Annie Pilchard survived to trial.

The search for Collick in Dunn Swamp was intensified. State troopers had found hip boots, a shotgun, and a pistol under the floorboards of Collick's home. Some of the posse members trucked horses to the swamp to cover a greater amount of ground and, after a certain area had been combed, the horses were rounded up and taken to another part of the swamp. Every man in the posse was well armed despite the belief that Arthur Collick had escaped the area or succumbed to the harsh weather. Some thought that Arthur might have jumped a train because a set of train tracks ran through one section of the cypress swamp. The authorities put out a bulletin to train stations and depots to look for a black man hitching a ride and police made regular checks at crossings.

A snowstorm descended upon the county early in the afternoon on Wednesday. The search posse and the police in the swamp were forced to take shelter from the blizzard. The search was cut-off and residents awaited the clearing skies. Gale winds of more than 40 miles per hour beat down on the homes and properties of the lower shore. Hardly a soul believed Arthur Collick was going to be found alive.

But he was alive or, at least, surviving. His limbs had gone numb and the feeling hadn't returned. Running on dead legs had hurt for a while, but now, he felt nothing, and that depressed and relieved him all at once. His skin had begun to look different too – chaffed, dry, and cracked. The palms, no longer yellow, were gray and the skin was beginning to peel away at his fingernails. His right hand, mangled from the posseman's rifle shot, had stopped bleeding. The scab was hardening as the temperatures dropped below freezing.

No food, no water, no shelter, and no help: Arthur knew he was going to die.

He had made his way out of the cypress swamp after the search parties abandoned their efforts the night before. Arthur didn't know why they all left, but he cautiously took advantage of their mistake. There was no doubt they would come back so he had to move. He passed through the backwoods as quickly as his feet of lead would allow and had made it as far as the woods just outside of Snow Hill when the winter storm stopped him.

Blinded by the torrents of snow falling on his wanted head, Arthur knew he had to find shelter or else be eaten alive by the blizzard. He dragged several small logs and branches, thickly coated in ice, to a little patch of earth nestled between a group of little pine trees. He cemented the cracks with packs of ice and snow. Once haphazardly assembled, Arthur Collick crawled inside.

Harvey Pilchard was dead, and for that, he was glad. He meant to do that. Three goddamn chickens cost him three years in that city prison. No one cared about Arthur Collick, the chicken-thieving black boy from the sticks. Mr. Pilchard got what he deserved, he thought. He had a thousand chickens up on that farm and a couple old ones weren't going to matter. What law makes a few chickens equal three years of hard time in prison? Arthur didn't know and he didn't care anymore. Arthur had already thought about it all too much anyway.

Besides, it was almost over. Harvey was dead and soon he would be too. Arthur had killed a white man and when the posse found him, they'd kill him. If the posse didn't find him, but the police did, then he'd either die in jail or be executed. And if the judge and jury and executioner didn't kill him, then it might as well be the blizzard that would pick his bones clean like a giant white vulture. Arthur Collick knew he was a dead man. Only two questions remained: when and how?

The winter storm raged on, beating the sides of the makeshift tent. Sharp stabs of pain from briar scratches deep in his skin and the bullet wound on his hand refused to let him sleep. His thoughts turned away from Harvey Pilchard. Now, the wife, Annie, was in his mind's eye. Her body had been so fat and warm, and he remembered watching her dark eyes grow large with fear. She had smelled like kitchen grease and wild flowers, just like a mother. Arthur Collick closed his eyes and half-wished he was already dead.

When the skies broke clear on Thursday morning, the search posse and police efforts were renewed in Dunn Swamp. Officers began visiting the homes of local black farmhands to see if he had taken up with any of them or to see if any of them had provided him with shelter. Every man expected – and wanted – to find Arthur Collick dead. The blizzard surely would have been too much for him to handle. A confident Maryland State Police officer told all the local papers, "If things go according to schedule today we'll be out of here by 5 o'clock this afternoon."

Even William Kerbin was certain of Collick's impending capture stating, that upon his capture and release into police custody, he intended to call a special grand jury session. Charges would be filed without delay and the courts were willing to grant the motion. The circuit court of Worcester County appointed another prosecutor, Godfrey Childs, to help William Kerbin prepare and expedite the case. Everyone knew Collick's capture was mere hours away, that is, everyone but Arthur Collick.

The five o'clock deadline came and past. Dusk fell on the county and disappointment was evident on the faces of the authorities and the citizens who kept all their doors and windows locked, shades drawn down, and guns loaded by their bedsides. Night came and Collick was still very much at large.

Tips and reports of sightings were reported all night to the authorities. They tracked every single lead. There was a desperate feeling in the white community and the police rushed to ease the nervousness, a rush that ended in false alarms and many mistakes.

Police officers in Baltimore City believed they had found the suspect after a black man was found with the initials "A.C." stitched into his clothing. He was immediately taken into custody for the murder of Harvey Pilchard. After the suspect's fingerprints were analyzed, the police realized their mistake. He was free to go because he was not Arthur Collick.

A black hitchhiker found in the back of a pick-up truck riding through Elkton, Maryland, was taken into custody by police officers, but he too was found to be without a connection to Arthur Collick and the Worcester County murder.

Police in Delmar, Delaware, apprehended a black man when he jumped off a northbound Pennsylvania Rail Road train. When police reviewed his Social Security card, he was identified as Freedman Miller and not Arthur Collick. However, the man was not released because he had trespassed on railroad property and was held on that charge.

No tip panned out; no sighting led to the true suspect. Confidence was fading. Many believed that he had succumbed to the elements, but no one had found a body. Sheriff Hall wondered if they would ever capture Collick, saying only a "lucky break" would do. No one quite understood how, in a blizzard, a poorly dressed man was evading capture by more than a thousand men with a thousand rifles.

Sheriff Hall was getting nervous. William Kerbin was still getting death threats at his home. Neither man could turn his back on the suspect or his own people. Arthur Collick became more than a man – he became a ghost, a legend, a mythic black magic devil. He was the focal point of every conversation, every telephone call and every gun in the county.

Still roaming the woods of Worcester County, the real criminal was unaware of his meddling in the lives of others. How could he know the impact his crimes were having on innocent people as far as 200 miles away? All Arthur Collick knew was that his stamina was growing as thin as his belly. The frenzy was all around him, but so far, it was not on top of him.

Around 10:30 p.m., Collick banged on the door of a small cabin that belonged to an elderly woman.

"Help me, please. I need food."

Frightened, the old lady tried to shut the door on him, "No, go away!"

Collick lunged at the door, throwing his whole ragged body into the motion. The door swung back and knocked the old black woman back. He entered the small cabin and shut the door behind him.

"I said, I want some food. That's all."

She gave him two biscuits with a little bacon grease. Lifting the biscuits to his nose, he took a long inhalation. "Thanks," he said as he opened the door and ran back into the night. She contacted the authorities and three carloads of officers arrived within minutes.

Collick knew the police would be coming soon. The old woman was sure to report him. He ducked into a nearby brush and quickly ate the little portion of food. The bacon grease remained on his lips; he couldn't wipe it away, and for a moment he was grateful just for the smell of it. He looked up the road and saw the cabin of Orphus Mills. Checking the road, Arthur made a run for it and began beating on the door.

"I'm all in," Collick yelled to Mills. "I want a place to hide."

"No! We don't want you. We don't need no troubles." Orphus Mills slid the bolt to block out the fugitive.

Just then, police headlights turned upon Collick standing in front of the little shack. Officers saw Collick. He froze in the sudden bright flood of light. But just as quickly as the lights came upon him, Arthur Collick jumped into the shadows and dashed off into the woods.

Local men, armed with guns and clubs, picked up the chase where they had left it just two nights ago. Eighty men were hand picked by the police because they had sworn that they would not lynch the fugitive if they caught him, but the men were never deputized. The search for Arthur Collick was revitalized and the men went forward into the cold, dark woods with the warmth of adrenaline and anger.

The posse was joined by 40 more state police officers and they formed a triangle around Girdletree. More local men joined the search but they worked independently of the main group. Three more sightings were received; Collick had knocked on more doors only to be turned away. Each time he escaped, he further infuriated his pursuers.

The difference between the pursued and pursuers was a matter of purpose. The posse's desire was to kill. Collick's desire was to live. His evasion was like a grand magic trick; he just vanished into thin air, even when they were right on top of him. Arthur Collick was always moving and always standing still, it seemed, always picking up just enough food to keep running and keep hiding. Nothing could trap him, but then, how does one go about catching the wind?

One of the state police officers fell upon an idea that would prove to be critical; they would use Collick's dog, King, to find his tracks. Friday, the authorities decided, was going to be the last day of the hunt.

At dawn, he turned up at a cabin of an elderly black couple. Holding his hand suspiciously over his pocket, Collick warned them he was carrying a pistol. "Feed me or I'll shoot both of you dead." The old woman started toward her pantry while her husband kept a nervous eye on the half-man, half-animal thing that had slumped down in a chair. Two muskrats were fried to perfection and Arthur Collick nearly swallowed them whole, ripping off large chunks with each bite and quickly pulling the little bones from his teeth with chapped fingers. As quickly as he ate, he rose to his feet. Neither the old man nor the old woman moved as Arthur Collick stood. A short moment passed and finally, he slipped out the door and into the night.

The two muskrats felt good on his stomach as empty as it was. He made his way back to Girdletree through the morning. Narrowly missing the white people patrolling the roads, Arthur Collick moved like a ghost, just in and out of plain sight. Once in a while he heard the airplanes buzz low over the trees and his heart pounded.

Come noon, Collick's luck was winding down. He turned up at the farm of Harvey Redden, one mile north of Girdletree. He crept up to the back door and saw their black cook standing at the stove.

"Psst, hey, you. Gimme some food out here."

The cook's eyes turned to the back door, and she screamed. Mrs. Redden ran into the kitchen and saw Arthur Collick moving toward the door. She yelled to the cook to ring for the police and ordered him off her property.

He turned and ran past the front of the house, crossed Snow Hill-Girdletree Road and disappeared into a small wooded area that only measured one square mile. When the authorities arrived a few minutes later, she pointed them in the direction of the woods. Accompanying the police were King, Collick's dog, and the Reverend Harry Nichols of Painter, Virginia – Annie Pilchard's brother.

King was turned loose at the back door. Immediately, he picked up his owner's scent and dashed into the woods. Men trailed Collick from the farmhouse to the woods. Meanwhile, state police officers formed a triangle and spread out – one band went west, another south, and the last east.

In the band that went east were three officers, Reverend Nichols, and the dog. They beat their way through the underbrush, trying to move as quickly as possible to keep up with the dog. King lost and regained the scent several times. When the group emerged from the woods into an open field, they saw the body of a black man lying face down about 20 feet from them.

The men drew their guns and crept up behind him. One of the officer shouted to him.

"Arthur Collick, get up with your hands in the air!"

The fugitive heard his name and knew it was over. He turned his head and saw the four men and his own dog. Slowly he picked himself up and turned to face them. The four men stared in silence as they examined him with disbelieving eyes.

Arthur Collick stood with his arms stretched out to his sides. His eyes were blank, brown marbles; his clothing was ripped and spotted with dark stains; his right hand was mangled, showing the mark where the posseman's bullet had hit him. The black skin held deep lacerations, some seemed fresh and others were scabbed over. The officers said nothing more to him. The reverend whispered something under his breath. The four men stared at the infamous fugitive of the cypress swamp. Arthur Collick was a dead man walking.

Still clutching his rifle, Reverend Nichols looked deep into the eyes of Arthur Collick, the man that raped his sister and left her for dead; the man that killed his brother-in-law; the man that was going to go to hell for all he had done. The Reverend wrestled with himself: should he be desirous of this man's death? Or should he relieved that he was alive and in custody? His role as a brother and as a religious man was blurred by images of Arthur Collick torturing his family and by the blood that stained almost every inch of his body. There would be no reconciliation standing there in the frozen potato field; the Reverend seethed with hatred, his fist clenched so hard around the gun barrel that his knuckles wanted to break. All he saw he detested, and in turn, despised himself wholly for it.

An officer stepped forward and searched him. The hat in his back pocket had a bullet hole through it.

A loaded .32 caliber revolver rested in his trouser pocket. Looking Arthur squarely in the face he said, "You're under arrest for the murder of Harvey Pilchard."

Offering no resistance, Collick looked at the four men in front of him and he spoke.

"I'm glad it's over."

Once the word got out that Arthur Collick had been captured, mobs formed in the streets of Pocomoke – a final but futile effort.

They sped through Snow Hill at high speeds to get to Bridgeville, Delaware, where Collick was remanded to a police car. His final destination was the jail in Bel-Air, Maryland, but there was one more stop. The car pulled over in Elkton, Maryland, at the request of William Kerbin. He wanted Collick to undergo a physical exam, which could be presented as evidence at the trial.

The official report to William Kerbin stated that Arthur Collick was "free from injuries, marks, and scars that might indicate any violence to his body."

Arthur Collick began to weigh his situation carefully as he was taken to Bel-Air. He told the police he wanted to talk, and proceeded to blame the murder of Harvey Pilchard on Charles Manuel. He admitted to attacking Annie Pilchard, but said Charles Manuel shot her too. Could he push the blame to Charles Manuel and spare his own life? The police officers were uninterested in his side of the story. He persisted and they ignored him.

Collick was served with a warrant charging him with the murder of Harvey W. Pilchard when he entered the Bel-Air jail. The warrant had been flown to Baltimore and then driven to the jail to be hand-delivered. William Kerbin had wasted no time in ensuring the expedition of the trial and he would not rest until each procedure had been followed to the letter.

Collick's capture was met with joy, relief, and a special conference held late in the afternoon on Saturday. The three Worcester County Circuit Court judges assembled in private chambers to discuss whether or not the accused would stand trial in that county or allow a change in venue.

Because of the attack on the jail, the death threats received by Kerbin, and the unstable atmosphere of the southern portion of the Eastern Shore, the judges ruled it was in the best interest of the accused to turn the case over to the judges of the Baltimore County Circuit Court. However, the indictments would be delivered on the shore. They granted William Kerbin a quick court date for the special session of the grand jury to make his case for indictments against Arthur Collick, Charles Manuel, and George Selby. The date was set for February 27, 1940.

The special session of the grand jury met at 10 o'clock in the morning on the 27th of February 1940. More than 200 local residents filed into the courtroom to watch the case while twenty-three men, pulled from the streets of Snow Hill, were sworn in as the jurors. After a roll call of the jury, the court delivered its orders to the jury.

Judge James Crockett charged the jury with the crimes related to the attack at the Pilchard farm, but he focused most of his 15-minute speech on the mob violence and the attack on the jail. "If our information is correct, it must be evidence of the acts mentioned should not escape attention by this court or the culprits go unpunished. The participants in this affair are not entitled to be held blameless. Impelled by anger and frenzy they ceased to exercise reason and judgment and not only defied the law but violated the rights and damaged the property of others and in addition they committed acts calculated to thwart justice."

"We have read statements appearing in newspapers which indicate the officers have information as to the identity of certain persons implicated and we suggest that you call before you all officers who had custody of said prisoners or who came into contact with the mob and this Court urges you, the Grand Jurors, that in this matter you be not remiss in your duties." Crockett aimed every word directly into the faces of the Grand Jury. The hearing had begun.

William Kerbin brought forward a total of eight witnesses, including Sheriff Hall, Martha Blake, Virginia Lillian Blake, local physician and Worcester County Medical Examiner John L. Riley, and other law enforcement officers to build his case against the two Negroes. Although Arthur Collick and Charles Manuel were kept in Baltimore County, the Blake women were specifically brought back to the shore for their crucial testimony. The most important witness of all, Annie Pilchard was unable to appear because her physician said she was in no condition to testify. William Kerbin desperately wanted to move quickly, but the grand jury hearing would have to proceed without her. Because the jury members were picked at random from the streets of Snow Hill, he remained confident that his jury would pass along the necessary indictments.

Kerbin's family was still being threatened and he slept with a gun next to his head. The death threats on his wife and children weighed heavily on Kerbin's mind. As an unspoken rule of thumb, to end it all, Collick and Manuel had to be indicted. William Kerbin, although tired and frustrated, strode into the courtroom and masterfully presented his case to the jury.

With the testimony of Kerbin's witnesses and the judge's opening charges, the grand jury went into deliberation, but the recess only lasted a few minutes. The Grand Jury returned to deliver its report. The judges called the court to order and the foremen announced the indictments.

Arthur Collick and Charles Manuel each received indictments for murder, armed robbery, and assault with attempt to kill. Collick alone received an indictment for rape. Despite attempts by the prosecution to implicate George Selby as a lookout, the jury did not indict him with any charge related to the event. The evidence did not warrant it, and he was free to go.

As for the mob attack on the Snow Hill jail, the Grand Jury report made absolutely no mention of it. The court adjourned.

As spring crept up on the Eastern Shore, the arraignment date for Arthur Collick and Charles Manuel was announced: March 14, 1940 at the Baltimore County Circuit Court in Towson, Maryland.

The day before the arraignment, Sheriff Hall drove over to the western shore to personally move the prisoners from the Harford County Jail in Bel-Air. Once the notorious prisoners were in place at the Maryland State Penitentiary, the Baltimore judges ordered that armed guards be placed on 24-hour standby at both Collick and Manuel's cells. The judges had heard about the jailbreaks in Worcester County, and were not going to allow such incidents to take place under their rule.

The prisoners were going to remain exactly where they were jailed.

On the day of the arraignment, armed guards, deputy sheriffs, and city policemen led the two prisoners into the large courtroom filled with dozens more officers and about 75 spectators, most of whom were Baltimore residents. The prisoners stood next to their appointed defense counsel: L. Paul Ewell of Pocomoke for Arthur Collick and William H. Price of Snow Hill for Charles Manuel.

The audience rose to its feet as the three robed judges marched in and took their places above the heads of Arthur Collick and Charles Manuel. The accused remained standing as the long indictments against them were read.

"How do you plead to these charges against you, Arthur Collick?"

"Innocent."

"How do you plead to these charges against you, Charles Manuel?"

"Innocent."

Their pleas were noted.

William H. Price asked for a severance of trials because evidence specifically used against Collick might taint the case against Manuel. The judges considered the motion and would deliver their decision on the first day of the trial.

The defendants were content with the change of venue, but not because they had any hopes of being freed. Simply, they knew there was no hope for a fair and impartial trial on the Eastern Shore. They didn't want to imagine a court filled with mob members and their wives and children, all staring holes into their backs. But, then again, Baltimore City was just a different set of white folks.

Kerbin addressed the court, asking for a delay in the trial date because their main witness, Annie Pilchard, resided in a hospital in Wilmington, Delaware. She wanted to be close to her daughter while she recuperated from her injuries sustained the night of the vicious attack. The court agreed to postpone the setting of the trial date to wait for the witness.

The waiting began.

July was one of the hottest months on record; temperatures soared to nearly a hundred degrees. In the month that seemed to radiate from hell, the hot-tempered case against the two Worcester County Negroes accused of one of Maryland's most vicious and indecent crimes went to trial.

On July 29, 1940, the three-judge panel of the Baltimore County Circuit Court began proceedings. The first order of business was the motion for the severance of trials, asked for by Manuel's defense attorney, William Price.

Prosecution argued against the separation of the trials. Kerbin cited that Worcester County would be forced to pay many witnesses $12 each per day and many would have to be reimbursed for driving from Worcester County to Towson – a one-way trip of 200 miles – and then home again. But the Western Shore court disagreed with the young state's attorney. The court argued, "This is a serious case and no doubt some evidence against one defendant might not be properly admissible against the other. Having that in consideration and to resolve any doubt in favor of the defendant, we grant the severance."

Two trials were set before the court and both defendants refused their right to a jury trial. The judges dismissed the jurors until the sentencing phase. Arthur Collick would stand trial first. Court adjourned.

Outside the courtroom, Kerbin issued statements to the newspaper reporters. "Identical evidence had been prepared against both men," he said. "The state witnesses are the same and from what I can learn the witnesses for both defendants will likely be the same," he said. Kerbin's star witness, Annie Pilchard, was finally able to testify.

In the opening statement of Arthur Collick's trial, Kerbin's assistant, Godfrey Childs, laid out the prosecution's intentions. Childs said the State sought to prove that the two men deliberately committed the crime, and that he would expose the premeditation. The first day brought forward a damaging witness – Virginia Lillian Blake.

That Sunday night, she said, Arthur Collick and Charles Manuel dressed in overalls and hip boots and left the house. When they returned later that night, they looked scared and hid their guns and boots under the floor.

"I said to Arthur Collick, 'Arthur, I heard a gun shoot.' He said, 'No, I haven't heard a gun shoot.' And I said to him, 'Arthur, what's the matter?' And then he said he killed Mr. Pilchard and Charles Manuel shot Mrs. Pilchard."

Godfrey Childs pressed the Blake girl; "Did Charles Manuel say anything?"

"No, sir." She replied.

"What did Charles Manuel do?"

"He just kind of held his head down."

The State revealed the boots and guns to Virginia Lillian for identification. Prosecutor Childs held the shotgun up for the young girl to see. "What shotgun is that?"

"I don't know."

"I don't mean the make. I'll put it another way. Have you seen this shotgun before?"

She answered, "I have seen it before."

"When?"

"I saw it that Sunday night."

"What Sunday night?"

"February 10th, maybe 11th."

"When you saw it, who had it?"

"Arthur Collick." The blame was laid.

"Where did he get it from?"

"From over our front room door."

The state admitted into evidence the shotgun, two pistols, a cartridge belt, and two pairs of rubber boots. The defense objected, but they were quickly overruled. Childs had no more questions for the young girl. Collick's lawyer, L. Paul Ewell, did not question the young girl and she was quickly excused.

The Worcester County Medical Examiner, Dr. John L. Riley, was the next to take the stand. Riley gave his testimony: Harvey Pilchard was killed by a shotgun blast to his abdomen. After the shot, he lived for a few minutes and then expired on the living room floor. Annie Pilchard, he said, suffered a severe gunshot wound to her back and there was sufficient evidence to indicate a sexual assault.

Again, Ewell had no questions for the doctor. Not a single question. The doctor was excused.

As the trial proceeded into the afternoon, the July from hell quickly began to permeate the room. Stifling heat in the crowded courtroom forced the three judges to remove their black robes, a break in judicial tradition. Sweat beaded up on the head of the accused; rings formed under the arms of the attorneys who had removed their suit jackets. Spectators fanned themselves with newspapers and hats. The tension increased as the last witness of the day was called – Annie Pilchard. Eyes of the audience members darted from Annie to Arthur Collick and back as she quietly took the stand to recount the events of Sunday, February 11, 1940.

William Kerbin's moment awaited him on the stand. This testimony was going to be absolutely crucial to the trial and to his reputation in Worcester County. Annie Pilchard was his proof.

He approached her with confidence and reassurance, "I'm sorry you're having to go through this. We'll make this as quick as possible."

Annie's low voice thanked him, and she kept her eyes focused on him.

"Mrs. Pilchard, can you please tell the court what occurred in your home the night of February 11?"

Annie maintained a steady gaze on William Kerbin because, to her, he was as mighty as God in that moment. He was Annie Pilchard's great avenger.

As she started to speak, her voice trembled. She could feel Collick's eyes on her again, like his stare was crawling up her arms and down her back. She knew he was watching, but she refused to meet his dark eyes.

"Mrs. Pilchard, can you tell the court what happened the night of February 11?"

"Yes."

"Go on," Kerbin softly urged her. Annie began to tell her story. She told the judges that she was writing a letter and listening to the radio when a knock came at the back door.

"I heard a shot and I ran to the kitchen. And Harvey," she broke off. "Harvey was..." Her sobs silenced the courtroom. Kerbin told her to take her time. The court waited. Annie gathered herself as best she could; she no longer felt the eyes on her skin.

"And he was shot. Then Arthur Collick rushed in behind him." She continued on with her testimony until Kerbin asked her about the attack.

"Mrs. Pilchard, what happened in the hallway?"

No words were spoken. Annie's red eyes closed and tears rewet her face. The court was completely silent. Then very quietly, almost inaudible, she whispered, "He…attacked…me."

Arthur Collick looked down at his hands.

Kerbin maintained his steady course, asking her about the money and the moment she was shot. The new line of questioning was a little easier for Annie Pilchard. Still, no one looked at Arthur Collick.

She testified that as she removed her purse from the bureau, she was shot in the back. She said it was Collick who shot her and then they both left her for dead. When she came to, she said she heard "more than two" sets of footsteps coming up the stairs, and so she escaped out of the window.

"I heard the men leave but then they came back, yelling at each other, 'Did you see her?'"

Kerbin asked a few more questions about being rescued and the extent of her injuries and then he rested. As he sat down, his eyes remained fixed to the woman on the stand. A rapidly aging woman, a widow, a victim, and a mother – who was Annie Pilchard now?

Annie was growing weary. The humid atmosphere hung about her neck and shoulders. She took comfort in the young prosecutor's constant stare, especially as Collick's attorney, L. Paul Ewell stood up.

"We have no further questions, Your Honors." Annie was finished. She never had to say Arthur Collick's name again.

Collick's trial ended abruptly when his lawyer decided not to offer any rebuttal testimony from a witness or Arthur Collick. The decision was made earlier in the day after Virginia Lillian Blake said that Collick had admitted the crime to her and showed her $18 in miscellaneous change after he discarded the evidence under the floor boards. For Ewell, there was nothing left to say, nothing to refute.

The case against Arthur Collick was rested; the judges reserved the verdict until after the trial of Charles Manuel, which was set to begin the following morning. The judges strode out of the room and the bailiffs returned the men to the jail. Annie Pilchard, surrounded by her daughter and family members, was helped out of the courtroom. The other attorneys filed out after brief handshakes and small, personal deliberations among themselves.

Arthur Collick was angry. Why wasn't his lawyer asking any questions? Faced with the cold reality of his situation, Arthur took matters into his own hands.

"Guard! Guard! I swallowed some glass!"

The guard ran to Arthur's cell and found him kneeling on the floor of his cell. He had one hand wrapped around his neck, and the fingers on the other hand were digging at the back of his throat, clawing and pulling. He was gagging and spitting on the floor in front of him.

"Help me!" His eyes looked as though they were going to pop out of his skull, and tears ran down cheeks. The guards opened his cell and grabbed him by his arms.

Collick gagged and coughed, spit and choked. The guards dragged him by his arms to the prison physician.

During the examination, the doctor reported finding no indication of injury and the guards reported that they did not find any glass in his cell. Arthur

Collick was taken directly to the courtroom for the start of the trial against Charles Manuel.

Kerbin called forward witnesses who testified that the size and marking of footprints found on the sandy loam outside the Pilchard farm corresponded exactly with boot prints inside the house. Two police officers testified that trademarks on heel prints were identical with those on the boots found underneath the floorboards in Collick's house.

Charles Manuel's lawyaer, William Price, sought to establish an alibi for Charles Manuel's whereabouts that Sunday night. He produced five different witnesses who said his client was at the Blake residence from 7:30 p.m. to 9 p.m. The attack at the farm took place a little after 8:00 p.m.

But Kerbin would not be outdone. He put two rebuttal witnesses on the stand who each testified that Manuel did not come home till 8:45 p.m. and then left again 20 minutes later.

Price tried again. He produced a birth certificate showing that his client was only 16 at the time of the murder, making him a minor under the law. On August

5, 1940 – just days away – Charles Manuel would turn 17. The birth certificate would mean the difference between life and death.

The last witness of the day was, again, Annie Pilchard who gave almost the exact same testimony. She and the prosecution made reference to the rape, but Price objected. That, he stated, was not evidence against Manuel, but against Collick. The court agreed and she was not allowed to make any further reference to the rape.

When Kerbin was done, Price approached the witness stand. He too apologized for her situation and stated he would be brief.

"Can you point out the second man?"

She hesitated.

"Mrs. Pilchard, can you identify the second man who was in your home the night of February 11?"

"No, not directly."

"What do you mean?" The defense attorney carefully pressed her.

"I didn't get a good look at the other man. I couldn't see his face."

Annie could not say with any degree of certainty that Charles Manuel was the man who entered her home with Arthur Collick. The primary witness could not place Charles Manuel at the scene of the crime. The defense had stumbled across a viable alibi in the primary witness, and other witnesses called previously had placed him away from the crime. But like the others, the defense attorney from Worcester County knew the price of protection.

"Thank you, Mrs. Pilchard. No further questions." With that, Price rested Charles Manuel's case.

On the first day of August, the trials were over and the court reassembled for the delivering of the verdict. As the three-judge panel of the Baltimore County Circuit Court entered the room, Annie Pilchard held her daughter's hand. Other spectators held their breath as they awaited the final words of the notorious case.

"Before this verdict is read, have you anything to say?"

Neither man spoke.

In the case against the minor, Charles Manuel, the verdict was guilty. Chief Judge C. Grason narrowed his eyes on the boy, "You are to be immediately enrolled into the Maryland State Penitentiary to begin serving a life sentence for your crimes in this case."

The court stated that his age and the fact he was led by an older man saved him from receiving the death penalty.

The attention turned toward Arthur Collick, chicken thief, rapist, and murderer. Chief Judge C. Grason delivered the verdict: guilty. He delivered the sentence on Collick's head without hesitation: "You shall be hanged by the neck until you are dead, and may God have mercy upon your soul."

Arthur Collick nodded, "Thank you."

The Pilchard family heard everything and said nothing.

Arthur Collick was assigned to a cell on death row in the Maryland State Penitentiary on August 2nd, 1940. Only nine months had passed since his last stay in the prison, but this time, he knew, would be much shorter than three years. He waited almost a week before Governor Herbert O'Conor signed his death warrant.

The papers were presented to Arthur Collick: he would hang at midnight on Friday, September 13th, 1940.

Soon, it would all be over.

Flanked by prison guards and the jail chaplain, Arthur Collick walked into the Maryland State Penitentiary death chamber in front of more than 70 spectators. He never said a word to anyone as he walked up the 20-foot platform raised above the witnesses. The warden watched him mumbling a prayer with the chaplain as the executioner slipped a hood over his face.

At two past midnight, the trap sprung on Arthur Collick, a young Negro sharecropper with a bizarre criminal record. His black dangling body reflected in the wide eyes of the spectators. Many were simply curious and wanted to know, what does a dying man look like? Can you actually see the whole process from breathing to extinguishing?

Fourteen and a half minutes of utter silence passed. The prison physician stepped forward and placed a stethoscope over Collick's bare chest, listening to his heart. All was still. The doctor stepped back at

12:17 a.m. and announced to everyone present that Arthur Collick was dead.

Nearly two hundred miles away, the people of Worcester County slept. William Kerbin and his family, Sheriff Hall, the mob members, and the ordinary folks of small towns and villages across the county – no one stirred. The morning would bring news of Arthur Collick's death and everything would almost be as it was before.

That is the way of justice.

The warden revealed afterward that Collick had dictated a letter to be written to his sister. In the letter, Collick said, "'whatever she said was true". The reference was to the Blake girl, but no one ever doubted his guilt. Arthur Collick was charged but never tried on the rape count.

His accomplice, Charles Manuel was paroled in 1955, fifteen years later. He returned to the Lower Eastern shore for a brief period but he disappeared and no one ever knew what happened to him.

Less is known about the circumstances of Martha and Virginia Lillian Blake. No one was ever arrested for kidnapping them from the jail.

Annie Pilchard never returned to Worcester County; her home and its contents were sold at auction. She moved to Wilmington, Delaware, to be near her daughter. When her daughter died in the early 1980's, Annie moved to Memphis, Tennessee where her grandson lived. She resided at the Kirby Oaks Guest Home for several years. On December 10, 1989, Annie Pilchard passed away at the age of 102 – the bullet still lodged in her chest.

The Pilchard farmhouse still stands on the main road between Girdletree and Stockton. It belongs to someone else now. Few people remain who know what happened there more than sixty years ago.

William G. Kerbin, Jr. and his wife raised two children, a daughter and a namesake son. Five years after the murder, he purchased The Democratic Messenger, the very paper that reported so much of the Pilchard story. Kerbin finished his appointment as the Worcester County State's Attorney in 1946, but he never forgot the notorious case that helped make his career, and he never forgot the threats on his family. The state police lived with them for the eights months following the Pilchard murder, and Kerbin carried that .32 pistol for more than a year.

As he passed into his silver years, he still practiced law in Snow Hill. Every morning, shopkeepers in the historic downtown could see Kerbin's silver Lincoln Town Car in its resting spot on the corner of Bank and Green Streets. He remembered the murder as one of the most famous cases he ever tried, but some of the lesser details had begun to escape him. Kerbin didn't know where Arthur Collick was buried or if he was sorry.

Kerbin recounted the events of the case nearly sixty years after it happened: "Neither the Sheriff or myself knew anybody in the mob. We couldn't press charges if we didn't know the men." The men were local boys, probably members of the Grand Jury or the Grand Jury audience, probably the callers who left death threats at his home, probably his neighbors and his friends.

In the end, all that surrounded this terrible tragedy has been fading steadily over the decades. The newspaper clippings that detailed each moment are yellow and fragile. They have been placed in scrapbooks and hidden away in closets and desks. They are reminders that, sometimes, not everything is forgotten.

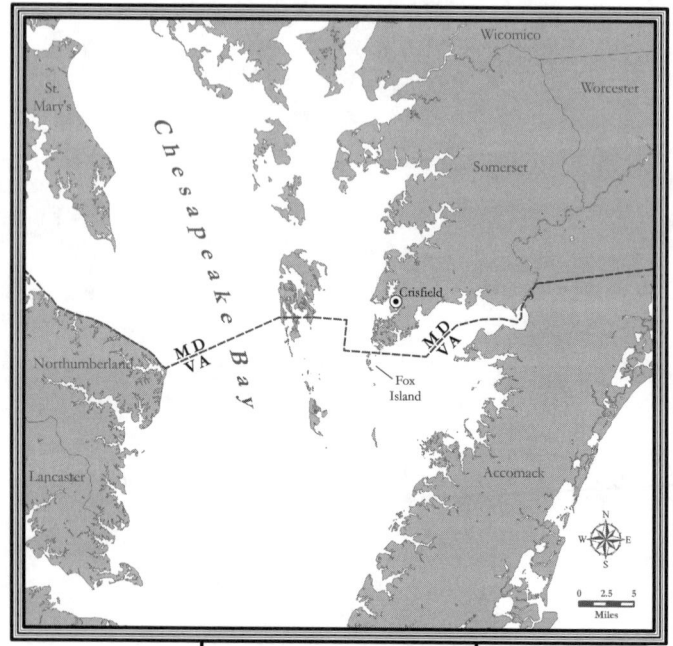

Lower Chesapeake Bay

SONS OF THE CHESAPEAKE

I

Orphans by the Bay

John Paul Nelson was 11 that summer of 1949. The boy was a true son of Crisfield. His blonde hair, nearly white, was cropped short to the back of his tan neck and his thick accent held slight intonations of the Smith Islanders who still spoke in near perfect and antiquated Shakespearian English. The July days were humid, but for the little white-haired boy, the days were as long as they were hot. Three months earlier, he had lost his mother to tuberculosis and life seemed to be vacant of happiness. The heat of the morning of July 5th eased just enough for John Paul to play baseball in the streets with the other neighborhood boys.

His mother was pregnant when she got sick. The doctor said that the baby had pushed against her lungs and that slowed down the disease, but once the baby girl was born, it took control of her body and she slowly began to die. Life at home was difficult for John Paul. His father, Earl Sr., spent his time divided between tending to his sick wife, caring for the baby, and going to work. Like many other men who lived in the Chesapeake Bay region, Earl was a waterman, but for several years, he was also a Crisfield police officer. He put in many hours on the water and did his best at home with his three children: John Paul, David, who was four years old, and the baby. John Paul spent most of his time watching over David, but still, John Paul was alone with a dying mother, a busy father, and siblings too young to know any better. In early April, she was gone.

After the funeral, Earl Sr. needed help. He was 50 years old, his wife was gone, and his children were suffering. His oldest son, Earl Jr., offered to take the baby girl, Dorcas, back home to Brooklyn, Maryland, to care for her until his father got back on his feet. Earl Sr. agreed and his daughter left Crisfield a few days after the funeral.

When his mother passed, John Paul, the fourth of six children, all but muted himself. He rarely spoke to anyone as he tried desperately to mend himself. His older brothers, Earl Jr., Gene, and Royce, did their best to make their beautiful brother smile. When they came for visits, they took him to the docks to fish, but all John Paul could remember was his mother's wasting away. Earl Jr. and Royce had not been there to witness her dying. Earl Jr. was married and lived far away and Royce lived near him. Gene had come home from the military in 1947, and lived nearby, working odd jobs around the small town and helping his father watch over the two youngest boys. John Paul took comfort in the visits of his older brother, but the older boys didn't know what she had looked or what she sounded like in the middle of the night, when he feared they would all die with her. They had not seen her pale and wasted, unrecognizable as their mother; they had not seen her pillows and nightgowns and sheets speckled with red spots. John Paul saw everything.

The passing of his mother had interrupted the natural flow from spring to summer. Gene helped around the house and did his best to lighten John Paul's spirits, but Gene was a strong-willed young man whose own life took most of his attention. The brothers, unfortunately, never talked much and John Paul felt alone in the small house full of sad men and unhappy children.

Three months after his mother's death, John Paul was beginning to welcome the warm days like July 5th because he finally got a chance to just be a boy again. About noon, the baseball game was well underway on a familiar side street. A skinny boy with red hair and burnt brown freckles ran up to John Paul and yelled, "Somebody's shot your daddy!"

Earl Nelson had gone out on his 26-foot scraping boat early that morning to go crabbing. Like most men of Crisfield, Nelson worked the bay waters to help feed his family. The little bayside village was literally built on top of oyster shells and the people of the town were intimately acquainted with their waters. They understood the Chesapeake's tides and lived by a stoic code of work, water, and time. This is the spirit of Crisfield.

Earl navigated the choppy waters of the Chesapeake to a familiar crabbing spot near Foxe's Island in the Pocomoke Sound, a place that lies dangerously close to the invisible boundary line between Maryland and Virginia. Being sure to stay in Maryland waters, he kept his boat running to the north side of the island. There he settled in for a morning of harvesting blue crabs from the endless bay.

There were other watermen out on the bay. The early morning was warm and sunny, a waterman's delight. Many others had motored out to crab near Foxe's Island. It was a dangerous place because of its geography. Marylanders and Virginians have feuded for years over the state line that cut an invisible jagged line through the dark waters of the Chesapeake Bay. Neither side wanted the other to sneak across the border and steal oysters, crabs, fish, and clams. Yes, Foxe's Island was a dangerous place to be, but the crabbing was excellent.

Earl had been on the water for about two hours when he noticed a mechanical buzz overhead. A seaplane circled over his boat, and landed fifty feet away. Earl watched as the plane turned towards Royce Sterling's boat. He watched as a deputy boarded the boat and took command, then headed off toward Virginia. Earl Nelson knew exactly what was going on – the Virginia police were arresting the Maryland watermen and taking their boats to Saxis, Virginia.

He started the motor and began moving closer toward the Maryland shore in case those Virginia boys wanted to confiscate his catch and boat. Just as Earl was moving north in the Pocomoke Sound, the seaplane turned and began advancing toward him.

He knew he could never outrun the plane. Earl just watched it as it chugged across the waves. As the seaplane approached, the words "Virginia Fisheries Police" were clearly visible on its metal side.

The seaplane carefully sided up to Earl's boat and a young deputy opened the tiny metal door. Holding a rifle, he boarded Earl's boat.

Earl took a deep breath. Above the mechanical churning of the seaplane, Earl said, "What can I do for you?"

The deputy stood in the center of Earl's boat. His hard eyes scanned the boat and locked on the bushel of crabs. "You can turn your boat off and put back your catch."

"Why? What's the problem?" Earl studied the man on his boat. His uniform tag read, "Acree". He could see that there was another person inside the seaplane, probably the pilot.

"I can see from your boat numbers that you're a Marylander. These here are Virginia waters, and I'm givin' you an order to turn this boat off and put back that catch." His eyes narrowed on the 50-year old Crisfielder.

Earl said nothing. He pulled a handkerchief from his back pocket and wiped his brow. The sun was beginning to burn him.

"We're goin' to Saxis, Virginia. I'm confiscatin' this boat."

A hearty laugh burst forth from the round chest of Earl Nelson. He knew he was in Maryland waters. If he let Acree take him to Saxis, he knew he'd lose his boat for sure and be fined heavily in the process. Losing his boat would be devastating for his family.

"Something funny?" Acree shifted his weight back and forth. His dark hair and chiseled jaws gave him the look of a strong canine.

Earl continued laughing. "You've got to be kiddin' me, son. We're north of Foxe's Island. I ain't doin' a damn thing wrong. And you sure as hell ain't takin' my boat." He turned his back to the young deputy and moved closer to the wheel.

"I'm takin' this boat whether you like it or not." Acree's voice lowered in a growl.

"Get off my boat, kid," Earl yelled over his shoulder. "You know we're in Maryland waters."

Sweat beaded up on Acree's brow and slipped down his tanned face, cutting sharp angles on his cheekbones and chin. He shifted his weight again and again. His fingers slipped down the barrel of the gun and his sweaty palms rubbed against the hot metal. He stared at the back of the old crabber who had laughed in his face and defied his authority. Everything in him wanted to strike out in defense of his job, his state, and his manhood. Acree had served four years in the United States Navy on submarine duty, and he returned to the area to work, initially, as a crop duster. He had seen men like this hard crabber before, men who fought tooth and nail for the weather-beaten, financial sinkholes they called their boats. His Navy training and his duty to his job reminded him to stay focused, but something else bubbled up inside of him like air pockets escaping through hot asphalt.

"Listen, I am takin' this goddamn boat!"

"Like hell you are! You ain't a cop, just a little boy playin' around in a uniform!" Earl Nelson craned his neck to look at the stern of his boat where the Virginia boy now stood.

Nelson's words rang like a thousand hammers in Acree's ears. His chest tightened. Those words, over and over, *"Like hell you are...Like hell you are."* The old waterman was blatantly disrespecting his authority. How could he let that happen? "He called me *a boy, a kid.*" White reflections from the bay burned into his eyes, lighting the fuse of his short temper. Acree's rifle lurched forward, a shot rang out, and a bullet tore through the lower abdomen of Earl Nelson.

The force slammed the old waterman's body forward against the wheel, and he grabbed hold of it. His body slumped over the wheel and fell to the side. Earl put his hands over the conjoining space where his hip and groin met his abdomen; his eyes locked onto the deputy's hard face. Acree, without a word, stalked off the boat and jumped into the seaplane.

The blood rushed up between Earl's fingers and he heard the plane take off. Suddenly, the sun was the hottest he had ever felt. Earl closed his eyes.

Watermen near Foxe's Island had been watching the Virginia Fisheries plane with anxious eyes. The contentious feud made everyone nervous. Over the past couple of months, a few men had been shot over the same problem in the lower Potomac. Several watermen witnessed the shooting and rushed to Earl's boat. The first men to his boat were Todd Marshall and Calvin Marsh, Jr., both Smith Islanders. As they climbed aboard the boat, they found him bleeding from the front and back, and barely alive. Each man stared at the ghastly mess – Earl Nelson's blood stained the entire boat.

Calvin Marsh's boat was the fastest in the vicinity so the watermen put Earl Nelson on that boat while another waterman took over Earl's boat. Calvin Marsh cranked up his motor and raced toward Crisfield. Todd Marshall dropped to his knees and pressed his rough hands over the open holes in the crabber's body.

Earl Nelson opened his eyes. "Help me," he whispered.

The waterman nodded. He watched as Earl's sad eyes slowly closed and his barrel chest stopped rising. When the boat docked in Crisfield, Earl Nelson was pronounced dead, and his three youngest children were pronounced orphans.

John Paul and several of his friends raced on their bicycles to the Bradshaw Funeral Home, the place where his mother was kept before she was taken to the cemetery. If his daddy was dead, then that must be where he could find him. If his daddy really was dead, then he had to see for himself.

The front doors of the funeral home had large glass panes. John Paul's hands formed a periscope around his eyes as he peered in the front door. The place was so dark inside; he couldn't make out anything. A tall man with a dark suit opened the door, and asked John Paul if he needed something.

"Yes. Some Virginia policeman shot my daddy. And I'd...I'd like to see him."

The tall man explained as best as he could that his father was not there. He was sorry that he couldn't be of more help.

John Paul stared blankly at the tall man in the dark suit. If he wasn't inside lying on a table, then where was he?

The young boy looked familiar to him. "I'm sorry, son, I don't know how I can help you."

With that, John Paul simply turned and got back on his bicycle. "I'm gonna go have a look at my daddy's boat," he said mostly to himself. John Paul and the boys headed for the wharf.

When John Paul reached the docks, he saw his father's boat moored against the old wooden pilings. John Paul threw his bike down and ran to the edge, pushing his way through the crowd of men and straining his eyes in the bright sun to make sure his father was alive and well. But what John Paul saw that day on the docks changed his life forever.

His father's boat was awash in blood and, on the dock, his father lay like a carelessly gutted fish in the arms of another watermen.

More than 400 people attended the viewing of Earl Lee Nelson as all of Crisfield, Somerset County, and other local townspeople turned out to pay their respects. Two reverends and a full choir presided over his open-casket service. The six children were all present: Earl Jr. with baby Dorcas, Gene, Royce, John Paul, and David who had recently turned five years old. Each son took his turn at his father's side for one last time.

Earl Jr. held his baby sister in his arms as they both stared down at their father. When he walked away, Dorcas stared back at Earl's face. She was too young to know what had happened, and many thought it a strange blessing that she would never remember the tragedies of her parents.

David walked alone to his father's casket. He stood on the tips of his shiny black shoes to look into the casket at his father, and then, as though he understood everything, he turned to the choir with tears streaming down his face. No one moved as he turned back towards his father's casket. A little ledge provided him with footing enough to peer down inside. He nudged his father with his small hands like he was trying to wake him from a nap. At last, David pulled himself over the edge of the casket and curled up on top of his father's chest, his white-blonde head underneath his father's stiff chin. A lady came forward and picked him up out of the casket as he screamed for his dead father.

Then there was silence.

John Paul was the last to look. He slowly took each step to the casket. His mother had just been here, had just looked like this. When he reached his father for the last time, he felt something tear inside his young body. The onlookers watched as John Paul finally burst into tears and slumped over the casket. As grief pulled him to his knees, a few people rushed to the child and helped him back to his seat.

Nelson's best friend, an old Crisfield crabber, sang hymns as they closed the service.

When they arrived at the Sunnyridge Memorial Park where Earl was to be buried next to his wife, David was the first out of the car. Walking up to the burial site, David turned and asked, "What's all these pretty flowers for?"

His question was met with silence. Earl Jr. took his brother's hand and led him to the closed casket. The brothers stood close to each other, uncertain, devastated, and angry, with bowed heads as the last of their parents was lowered into the ground.

II

Drawing Lines in the Salt

The funeral of Earl Nelson was only the beginning of a tumultuous series of events. The murder sparked a heated flare-up in an old debate between the states of Maryland and Virginia that had been ongoing for more than 200 years.

Disputes over the property lines of each state date back before the signing of the Constitution. Fishing rights sparked the battle as both states claimed rights to the Potomac and Pocomoke rivers that separate them as well as the lower channels of the Chesapeake Bay. Simply, Marylanders and Virginians could not tell where the water ebbed from one state and flowed into the other.

With the brand new government joining together to forge a new road in the young nation's history, the battle over rights and lines had to be settled. Representatives from Maryland and Virginia met with General George Washington at Mount Vernon. There, the two states formed the Potomac Compact of 1785. The resulting compromise acknowledged Maryland's supreme ownership of the large river, but gave Virginia watermen the right to fish the Potomac. A terminus was established on each side of the Chesapeake Bay as a means for a primitive boundary line: Smith Point just south of the Potomac and Watkins Point near the Pocomoke. With this drawing, Virginia gained a considerable amount of oyster-filled waters. In return, Maryland received free access through Cape Charles. No longer would Virginia charge Maryland ships a toll just for passing through the mouth of the bay. The agreement also allowed violators of state fishery laws to be tried in their residential state, despite the location of their crimes. Maryland and Virginia representatives agreed to one last point: if either state made legislation regarding the river, both states would have to accept it or else the compact was nullified.

The Compact of the Potomac held until the Civil War when the states sided with different governments. When the war ended, there was still one unresolved question regarding the Chesapeake. It was a problem overlooked by the old compact formed on George Washington's table – where *exactly* was the state line between Maryland and Virginia that cut through the waters of the Chesapeake Bay? This question was at the root of the bitter hatred between Marylanders and Virginians and it was the very reason that the lower waters of the Chesapeake became a hotbed of violence.

Marylanders and Virginians vehemently disagreed about the boundary. The Compact of 1785 had not been specific enough for either side regarding the exactness of the line. There were acres of oyster beds and fishable waters to be gained or lost, depending on who won the line dispute, and each side held steadfast. Marylanders and Virginians, as much as they hated each other, had two vital points in common: neither would budge and both wanted a clear, definitive line. Where exactly that line was going to be drawn was the reason for their rivalry. Oysters and fishing rights could cause any man to turn on his neighbor – state, county, and street.

Finally, in 1877, federal authorities finalized the line in a deal known as the Black and Jenkins Award. Virginia won, by far, gaining huge amounts of water territories in the Pocomoke Sound as well as the Tangier Sound. Outraged and out of good oyster territory, the Maryland watermen demanded that the government in Annapolis intervene on their behalf. The watermen were completely isolated from their livelihood because, in the late nineteenth century, oysters were king of the Chesapeake. State officials were not eager to re-enter the battle with Virginia.

Watermen in Crisfield watched as Virginia watermen dredged the Tangier Sound, taking hundreds of their oysters and selling them in Virginian markets. To make matters worse, those same watermen often crossed the line of '77 to take oysters from Maryland-owned waters. Since help from Annapolis would not come, the Somerset County watermen decided to take action into their own hands. In December of 1883, Marylanders opened fire on every Virginia dredging vessel that entered their waters. In the late days of the nineteenth century, more than 50 men died and many more were injured in oyster feuds. No sooner had the Civil War ended than the war on the Chesapeake had begun.

Up and down the Chesapeake, there was gunfire and bloodshed, especially when the oyster boom of the 1880s hit. Watermen fiercely protected their rights and their beds. Each state went easy on its reported misfits and most troublemakers got away with a small fine and a proverbial slap on the wrist. Maryland and Virginia were not interested in punishing their own men; they were interested in crucifying the enemy. The harvests were rapacious; even oyster policemen were caught stealing.

In the 20th century, the boom halted and oystermen in the bay fell on truly hard times. The slim years on the Chesapeake were further compounded by harsh winters that froze the entire bay and by a hurricane in 1933 that flooded the salty bay with fresh water, nearly wiping out the oyster population. The competition was heated and desperate, and the oystermen were too proud to give up the only life they and their fathers had known. Oysters, rockfish, bass and clams all suffered the consequences and their numbers dropped off significantly. Still, Marylanders and Virginians alike were absolutely determined to make their living off the Chesapeake.

What evolved from this desire was the coronation of a new king of the Chesapeake – the blue crab. This crustacean caught the money-making eyes of Marylanders and Virginians as well as hungry markets that adored Mid-Atlantic seafood. Like the oyster, the blue crab would prove to be just another resource and one more reason for the two states to continue their battles.

The tensions mounted and the escalation pointed toward the worst possible ending – more bloodshed. Then, in 1949, came the murder of the Crisfield crabber, Earl Lee Nelson, Sr.

Because each state's authorities believed the crime happened in their waters, the shooting death of Earl Nelson lead to multiple trials, several warrants, and a chorus of angry watermen's outcries. The day after the shooting, the state's attorney of Somerset County issued arrest warrants for David A. Acree, 28, of Weirwood, Virginia, who was charged with murder, and George Colonna, the pilot, who was charged as an accessory to the murder. The newspapers reported that Acree was not on Virginia's state fisheries payroll and he had only been deputized four hours prior to the attack. When Maryland officials tried to serve their warrants, they were denied access to Acree. The Virginian authorities of Accomack County refused to allow Acree to fall under Maryland jurisdiction.

Two days later, David A. Acree appeared before the trial magistrate of Accomack County to answer Virginia charges of "feloniously killing and murdering" Earl Nelson. He pleaded not guilty and his bail was set at $10,000. A local farmer from Birds Nest, Virginia posted the bail and Acree was freed. Outside the courthouse, David Acree posed for the newspaper photographers and happily answered their questions, never once acknowledging the seriousness of his actions. He had total faith in the Virginia system.

Meanwhile in Maryland, the Somerset authorities worked hard for Acree's extradition. The Crisfielders wanted their day in court and they wanted Acree to pay with his life, either in death or in prison. A sympathetic ear was found in Annapolis as Governor W. Preston Lane flew to Crisfield to speak with the family and friends of Earl Nelson as well as to oversee the boundary survey near Foxe's Island that would help determine where Earl Nelson was shot.

Since there were warrants outstanding against Acree, Governor Lane asked the Virginia government and the Virginia Governor William H. Tuck to release the suspect into the custody of Maryland authorities so that warrants could be served and a trial could be set. Governor Tuck refused the request. The flaming disregard for the deceased crabber and his family, as well as for the disrespect of the line of '77, incensed the Maryland watermen and the people of Somerset County.

Acree's faith in the Virginia system proved well placed. His trial, due to the debate between the governors over the issue of extradition, was not held until August 15, 1949 in Accomack County. Witnesses from Virginia reported that a struggle occurred between Earl and Acree; witnesses from Maryland testified as to not having seen any sort of struggle aboard the 26-foot boat. Word for word, the story was a multi-faceted tale of state pride.

The jury did not return with a verdict, rather, they returned stating that there was no true bill for the crimes against Acree. The foreman, an insurance salesman from Onancock, Virginia, stated: "We, the grand jury, find that the shooting of Earl Nelson occurred in waters of Accomack County, Virginia. Further that the shooting was accidental, it having taken place when Earl Nelson attempted to snatch the gun from David Acree, and that David A. Acree was not guilty of any malicious act. Consequently, no true bill." He was immediately freed.

The verdict was precisely what the Marylanders had expected and feared. The editor of the Crisfield Times wrote, "Frankly, it was what I expected. I think the grand jury was exonerating the Virginia Fisheries Commission rather than just Acree. I think they were trying to get the State of Virginia out from under a civil suit that Nelson's family might bring." The community was outraged – a gentle, law abiding man had been shot in cold blood and three children were orphaned. The resonance of the verdict reached the Somerset watermen, already at odds with the Virginians. If it could happen to one of them, surely it could happen to them all.

In one final gesture that following September, a Somerset County grand jury indicted Acree on murder charges with the suspect in absentia. The gesture was understood, but the verdict was essentially worthless. Acree would never return to Maryland to answer to the charges. The case was over.

Watermen went back to the Chesapeake, only this time, armed with their own personal guns with one eye watching their catches and the other watching the enemy over the line.

III
Remains of the Day

As is the way of fate, nearly ten years after the murder of Earl Nelson, Virginia found herself facing a similar case. In April 1959, a Colonial Beach farmer named Berkley Muse and his friend, Harvey King, were dredging for oysters on the Potomac when they were spied by Maryland oyster police, who opened fire on them. Berkley Muse was killed in the exchange.

In a strange reversal, Virginians demanded the prosecution of the officers aboard the schooner that opened fire on the dredgers. Muse and those aboard his boat were unarmed and the amount of gunfire that they were subjected to was beyond fathomable. This time, Maryland was the state that refused extradition; however, the Maryland officers were punished under their own state's law. Virginia, although unhappy, had little say in the matter – the officers were punished and Muse was dead. Nothing more could be expected because one commonality of the two angry states was that the war over the Chesapeake and her invisible lines was growing tiresome and wasteful. Murder, finally, had become intolerable for both states.

The road to partnership was shakily underway; however, easing the centuries of hard feelings and bitter animosity between Marylanders and Virginians had already proved a most difficult, if not impossible, task. A bi-state commission to watch over the marine research of the Chesapeake Bay as well as seafood inspection was proposed. In 1962, President John F. Kennedy ratified the Potomac River Fisheries Commission. The governors of Maryland and Virginia joined the President in Washington D.C. for a luncheon, showing the public a warm welcoming of the new commission. Oysters on the half shell, quite naturally, were among the choice dishes served.

The signing of the bi-state commission legislation ended the war on the bay and life for Maryland and Virginia watermen finally settled down. Marylanders and Virginians alike were left to recall from memory the wild and destructive days of the past. For the families of the watermen who died in the wasteful war, the recollection was more painful.

The Nelson family was among those many families that were left behind when the war claimed their loved ones. Recovery from these high profile shootings was unattainable because with each new shooting, the scars had been ripped open, and with each new legislative movement the wounds were deepened.

The older Nelson sons were left to decide what must be done with their younger siblings. Earl Jr. and his wife decided to take Dorcas and raise her. Two children remained – two choices to be made.

The brothers were unsure about what to do with John Paul who was still suffering silently. For a brief time, he was placed in a foster home in Somerset County. Then he was sent to West Nottingham Academy near Rising Sun, Maryland, a private school that kept him largely isolated from his brothers. He spent most of his young life away from his friends in Crisfield and the comforts of a quiet life in Somerset County; his vacations from school were spent in Baltimore with his older brothers and baby sister.

Unlike his brothers, John Paul never recovered from the immediate deaths of his parents. As he grew older, the images of the bloody boat and his gutted father never left him. He was the most wounded of the Nelson boys. As though his emotional traumas manifested into physical ailments, John Paul had heart surgery and was diagnosed with cancer. His quiet nature stayed with him. John Paul Nelson died in 1990, unmarried and sick.

The only child left was David. Since Gene and Royce were unmarried and Earl already had Dorcas and his own children, no one could take care of David. The five-year-old boy became a ward of the state.

Not much time passed before David was placed in a foster home in Somerset County. The Weidemas were a wealthy couple with two adopted girls. Under their care, David, a shy and sad child, blossomed into a precocious and happy young boy. His transformation was remarkable and the road ahead of him looked good – for a time. He was soon told of his foster state, and he seemed to adjust well to the news. David vaguely recalled his former life; after all, the Weidemas had been the only parents he had truly known. But David's golden transformation would soon begin to tarnish.

As he grew older, the Weidemas desperately wanted to adopt David because they loved him as their son. Mr. Weidema couldn't buy him a car when he turned sixteen because David was not his legal son. A string of legal proceedings and court sessions held up the adoption and the final prevailing ruling was that David Nelson could not and would not be able to be adopted.

David could not understand why the Weidemas could not adopt him. Underpinning that confusion was a growing anger of not being wanted. One question burned in his heart and mind: who was he? Was he the orphaned son of a sick mother and murdered father who he could hardly remember? Or was he the son of two people unconnected to him biologically but who loved him deeply as their own? That the two Weidema girls had been adopted and that he would never be adopted only added to his misery. David's downfall began with those questions.

He enrolled in the Maryland State Police academy and became a state trooper. David married twice, and the second marriage produced three children. But long before the police academy, David wrestled with his demons and his never-closing wounds. In 1994, at the age of 49, he suffered a major heart attack and died. As though continuing a cursed legacy, he left behind three young children.

The children of Earl Nelson paid a heavy price. Gene Nelson died in 1990, the same year as John Paul. Earl Lee Nelson, Jr. died some years before them. The only two remaining are Royce and Dorcas. Royce maintained a relatively normal life with a well-adjusted marriage to a strong woman. Dorcas became a nurse in Baltimore.

The Nelson children never had a chance to heal because the murder was so publicized. They were stuck, helpless, in the middle of a well-known tragedy that had gained unprecedented notoriety, and the papers kept the wounds fresh with constant reports and interviews. Each child dealt with their scars in different ways; each had different demons to face. In the end, most everyone connected to the family knew only one thing – the wreckage left behind in the wake of Earl Nelson Sr.'s murder was borne of greed and killed by despair.

IV

The Invisible Mark

For centuries of time and generations of people, the Chesapeake Bay has been the central backbone of Maryland and Virginia's Eastern Shore culture. It has served as a means to making a living while awakening passionate loyalties that destroyed lives. So much has resulted from this body of water that lies in the middle of two states, with its arms and legs that stretch out at its sides and entangle the lands of Maryland and Virginia.

The watermen of the Chesapeake are a dying breed. Few men, if any at all, can recall the days when thousands of oyster rigs jammed the Tangier Sound, tonging for their fill of the sweet and salty shellfish. No longer do the watermen mount machine guns on their bows, ready to stake their lives for their harvest. Today, state regulations on blue crabs have made it all but impossible for watermen to continue pulling up their scrapes and pots and lines. Slowly, the watermen are giving up their boats and calling it a day on their careers.

We cannot comprehend this tragedy.

The sad desperate irony of their situation is that they have put themselves in this position. The bay's plentiful harvests were not going to last an eternity, yet the rapacious harvests continued with a seeming disregard for the future of their industry, and more importantly, the future of the Chesapeake. But this is looking through the eyes of a quiet observer. Restrictions and the sprawling urbanization of nearby farmlands, replete with sewer systems that interlock with the bay, are more of a threat to our Chesapeake than the dying watermen. The truth has been hard to see.

The remaining watermen of the Chesapeake Bay rise every morning and, on the bows of battered workboats, greet the dawn. Their lives are hard, but this is a right of passage handed down from their forefathers. But still they fight with hands thick with salt white calluses and their burned faces still carry the sun bleached beards of their grandfathers. Their loyalty to this never-ending work exceeds the length of light scattered by the waves, and their frustration with the looming end of their business will outlive even their grandchildren.

The waterman's life is hard and it is ruled by changing tides and legislative maneuverings. We often romanticize their way of life because it is an easy thing for a writer or a lover of the Chesapeake to do. How can we deny those men who give us the bounty of the Chesapeake Bay? How can we refuse those hands that haul crab pots and gut fish, those hands that build everything from crab sheds to boats to piers? It is easy to romanticize because we do not live that life ourselves. It is easy to love those who do what we cannot.

For centuries, the difficult struggle over the line revealed just how far Marylanders and Virginian would go for a simple crab or a simple oyster. When man opposes nature and his neighbor, what should we expect as the outcome?

The line in the Chesapeake remains an invisible thing. Decades of fighting and legislative dealings have not changed this. Today, no man can point to a breaking wave and say that it started in Maryland and broke in Virginia. Can anyone put their fingers in these dark waters and pronounce ownership? Can we justify killing a neighbor over a ghost?

And for this, our Chesapeake has been marked.

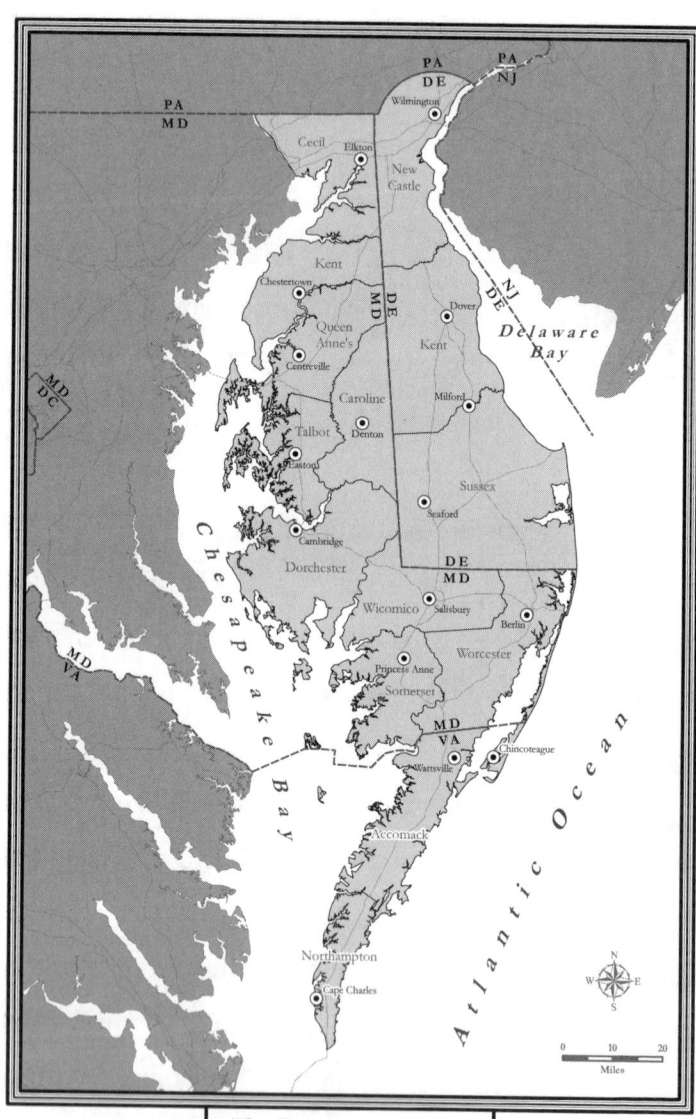

The Delmarva Peninsula

A Forgotten History

The forces of nature constantly change the physical landscape of the Delmarva Peninsula: tides, storms, and growing populations. But there is another force working equally as hard at changing the social landscape of this place – race. Maryland and Virginia were slave-holding states and they carry the marks of that institution. Segregation took its toll and change has been a slow process on this peninsula. History is still being written.

But for the children who grew up in that separated system, they are older now and they remember the way things were just a few decades ago. What is to be forgiven? What is to be forgotten, if anything? The hardships and challenges faced by so many children are unthinkable by modern standards. For the black children, frozen in time in old black and white photographs standing in front of a one-room schoolhouse, theirs was a story untold.

Until now.

There are voices among us. One will tell the story of the Sturgis One Room School Museum. Another will share the experiences of black students in Virginia. And two more will explain the trials and triumphs of teaching during the transition to integration.

Listen.

"We Shall Overcome"

On the corner of Willow and Front Streets in Pocomoke City sits a small, unassuming building known as the Sturgis One Room School Museum. Its whitewashed walls, blue trim, and gray roof bring life to its simple, single-story frame. The Sturgis One Room School is one of the last surviving African-American one-room school houses on the Lower Shore of Maryland, and perhaps one of the best preserved on the Delmarva Peninsula. To any passerby, this building is non-descript, but what lies inside is an uncommon history lesson.

On the other side of the door to the Sturgis One Room School Museum is a time machine. The wooden floors creak slightly under the weight of its visitors. In a far corner, two small black children – a girl and a boy – sit side by side at a desk. They do not move. A black teacher stands beside them. She does not move. The walls sconces are iron brackets precariously holding old-fashioned oil lamps. Daylight streams in through two windows on each side of the small school. To the right, there is a wood stove, a bucket of wood, and a little bit of kindling. At the front of the room, a picture of Abe Lincoln hangs next to a blackboard. When the front door shuts and the room is sealed from the interruptions of a modern world, the time machine begins a slow journey backwards and a history lesson begins to unfold.

Near the end of the Civil War, in 1864, Maryland legislators were hard at work on a new state constitution. This new contract would provide for public education, but not for the education of Negro children. The argument against providing education for black children was that it would breed a contentious desire in them to seek out political and social equality, a movement that was not deemed to be in the best interest of the state of Maryland. One lone politician from Baltimore spoke out in favor of educating black children.

This new constitution did, however, propose to abolish slavery in Maryland – a measure that was hotly contested by her lower Eastern Shore counties of Somerset and Worcester. Because Maryland was not a rebel state, the Emancipation Proclamation of 1863 did not free her slaves.

At the end of the war, the free black population realized that they needed many things very quickly, and among the most important of those were housing, employment, and education. The government recognized these needs as well and, in 1865, a welfare agency was established under the auspices of the War Department. The Bureau of Refugees, Freedmen, and

Abandoned Lands, or more concisely known as the Freedmen's Bureau, became involved in every aspect of their lives and dealt with complaints in all forms.

The Freedmen's Bureau had the increasingly important task of establishing Negro schools. On April 1, 1867, a Freedmen's Bureau official submitted a quarterly report to his superiors on the conditions of black educational interests in southern Delaware and on the Eastern Shore of Maryland. This was the officer's first report on Delaware since its addition to his district. He seemed very pleased that the pursuit of public education for black children was taking such a root in the state. Schoolhouses were being built and committees and associations were forming to see to it that this task was done. Initial tabulations of the black student populations put the number near 700. He wrote of Delaware's progress:

> *"The prospect in the State of Delaware for future success is very flattering – the enterprise is fully invigorated. ... The work so far as the Del. Assoc. is concerned is in the hands of very best men of the State, and the Bureau is co-operating with them earnestly and harmoniously to the full extent of its power. ..."*

But the optimism was short-lived. Less than one month later, in May 1867, a mob attacked and drove away the teacher of the black school in Georgetown. A field officer documented the scene in a letter sent to the Office of the Superintendent of Freedmen's Bureau.

> *"Sir, The opposition to the establishment of schools for colored people, which prevails in the lower portion of Delaware, has shown itself openly at Georgetown. A mob assaulted, and drove away, the teacher at the above place last Monday (27th) night. Understanding lumber was to [be] shipped for Milton, I decided to suggest delay in forwarding it until the difficulty above alluded to had been investigated. Milton is only a short distance from Georgetown, and the example set at the latter place may be followed at the former.*
> *Of course I write this on my own responsibility without authority from the association, but considering that I am doing my duty. There is a school established at Milton, and perhaps it would be better to wait and see if it meets with any opposition. In conclusion I would state that the association in connection with the loyal men at Georgetown will have the above outrage investigated."*

Similar problems were experienced in Milford, Delaware when a public meeting was held to discuss the opening of a black school in that town. Field officers from the Bureau met with townsfolk at a church to discuss the establishment of the school. Much to the surprise and chagrin of the officers, angry citizens worked themselves into a fervor over the issue. One official later noted the "violent opposition" in his report to the Superintendent.

Maryland was also lacking in her efforts to educate young black children. Negro churches on Maryland's Eastern Shore were burned because they had been used as makeshift classrooms. These arsons served as scorched reminders that Eastern Shoremen did not welcome the education of their labor force. Additionally, the schools faced troubles from other institutions that were, ironically, designed to help their cause. The Baltimore Association for the Moral and Educational Improvement of Colored People charged the rural schools fees for provisions and dues for membership. The Association was supposed to help provide teachers for the fledging institutions, but the demand for teachers was so great that many counties were stagnant in their progress. Thus, the end result was that most rural black children went without an education.

Of Maryland's problematic schools, the field officer wrote in an April 1867 report:

> "...We are much hindered in our work in this State by the want of teachers, as we have no authority under existing orders to pay teachers, and as the Balto. Ass. has failed to supply the demand, we have been unable to open schools in many places where applications have been made for the same – thus leaving in some cases whole counties without a single school, - others with but one or two, where there should have been a half dozen had we been supplied with the required number of teachers our schools would have been increased at least thirty percent since the commencement of the present school term...."

Later that same year, in 1867, a new constitution was written for the State of Maryland. Of the many provisions that stemmed from this new contract, several directly impacted the lower counties and their residents – black and white. First, a new county was formed on the Eastern Shore named Wicomico, after the river that ran through it. With the addition of Wicomico County, the Eastern Shore of Maryland consisted of nine counties. This new constitution gave black men the right to testify in court, and it also made provisions for the education of black children. However, these schools could only be financed by taxes collected from the black population, which meant for the poor backwater areas like the Eastern Shore, black schools would be, at best, meager.

More than a year later, Maryland's black schools were still experiencing problems with funding as well as staffing. The school report dated June 12, 1868, written by a Bureau officer, detailed the problems of the lower Eastern Shore schools.

"At Salisbury, Eastern Shore Maryland, I found that the school is now closed. It drew out from the Balto. Assoc. when it demanded the $15 monthly, and has since been conducted solely by the People. The people hope to re-commence, as soon as they can secure a teacher. ... At Princess Anne, Eastern Shore Md., I found the School reduced in numbers. The highest number present when I visited the school, only 19. The trustees seem to account for this decrease by laying the blame on the Teacher. The Teacher retorts by charging want of interest, upon the Trustees. The Teacher's salary is much behind but the Teacher and the people expect to hold a Festival to raise the amt. necessary. They seem united as to a School-House, and say that it shall go up without delay, and promise that the school shall be kept going. The deficiencies to the Salary of Teacher, is attributable to the demand of the Balto. Assoc. for the $15. It was 'the last feather which broke the

camel's back.' I propose, with Gen. Brook's order, to visit during my next journey, Talbot County, Kent, and balance of Somerset."

In Accomack County, Virginia, the Freedmen's Bureau was working on the establishment of schools for Negro children; however, the county's small size and low population made for slow progress.

On May 25, 1867, a black school was opened in Horntown, a small community in the northeast section of the county. At that time, there were only three known black schools in operation on the Eastern Shore of Virginia. The teacher at the Horntown school could not write, but her students were learning how to spell and read. Times were tough for this little school as interest in the school rapidly dwindled, and eventually, the teacher gave up hope. The parents of the nine pupils enrolled did not want to pay the extra fifty cents per month to keep the school running.

In September 1868, the Freedmen's Bureau gave $100 to Horntown to build a better schoolhouse. An official school report, dated December 1868, listed that project as unfinished, but the building was valued at

$250. Future predictions stated that, when it was opened, it could hold an estimated 60 pupils.

In that same school report, there is mention of an unfinished building worth $425 with a potential to house 80 pupils near "Chinchtown". There is no Chinchtown existing today, but it is plausible that this school may have been the beginnings of a black school near Wattsville on the road to Chincoteague Island.

Progress came slowly, but it came. On the Delmarva Peninsula, one-room schoolhouses began to appear all over the countryside. Both white and black children attended these modest and often ramshackle schoolhouses in which conditions for the white children were often only slightly better than those which existed for black children. Simply, many people of both races living in the rural parts of the peninsula were poor, and the conditions of the schools reflected the poverty of the community.

In 1895, there were approximately 18 black schools operating in Worcester County without the help of county-regulated funds. Maryland provided funds for public schooling for both white and black children;

however, the state provided more money for white pupils than for black pupils. Worcester County did not provide specific funds for the black schools; however, taxes levied on liquor sales to the black communities often went to support what schooling efforts had been established. The only evidence of the liquor tax financial support is a single document that was sent to the United States Senate, detailing how many black schools existed in Worcester County, how many students populated them, and how the schools were paid for.

In Worcester County, as typical of all counties in the region, the black school year was shorter than the white school year for the same reason. This held especially true for the children who attended the Sturgis Colored School.

It is unknown when the school was built, but the best estimation puts the original construction somewhere between 1888 and 1900. The one-room school was built on the property of the Sturgis family. The children who attended this school during the early 1900s were borne to farmers, field workers, fishermen, and people who worked in-service around Worcester County. The black school year started as late as mid-October or November and ended as early as the first days of April. To say the least, it was a haphazard attempt at schooling.

But there was one man who knew the power of education and he would not rest until black children were given more.

Stephen Long was born in Pocomoke, but grew up in Boston. When he eventually returned to the Eastern Shore, he began teaching. He was well educated and a fierce advocate of education. Long took particular interest in the issue that the children were not attending school but rather helping out in the fields and workshops in Worcester County. Immediately, he saw that the young black children were consistently absent from school.

Stephen Long started asking questions, too many questions. He made inquiries to law officials and farmers about the young black workers – the children workers – who, he believed, belonged behind rows of school desks, not rows of corn and wheat. Stephen Long was the first school supervisor for the black schools in Worcester County, and he made it his personal mission to see to it that the young black children received an education.

But local farmers grew agitated with Long and his questions and his mission with the children. There was a history between whites and blacks that dictated division and subjugation as a means of social safety and balance. Stephen Long was on the verge of upsetting that delicate balance.

On a hot mid-September day in 1921, two farmers caught him outside of a crossroads general store near Pocomoke City. They went inside and asked the proprietor if the man outside was Stephen Long, the man who wanted to change rules.

Indeed, it was.

The farmers walked out to confront him, ignoring the young girl by his side. A heated argument ensued between the farmers and Stephen Long about the black children. Each side held their ground, refusing to give up or give in. The conflict grew intense and heated. The hot summer sun did little to ease their agitation. Suddenly, one farmer struck Stephen Long. As he fell, the other struck him. Motivated by anger and hatred, the two men beat him to the ground with frenzied fists. While Stephen Long lay beaten on the ground, he was stabbed to death.

The two farmers might have gotten away with the horrible act had Stephen Long's own child, Jessie, not been the primary witness to the murder.

His death was a tragedy; his life had been cut short before his good works could become a reality. The school year that began in 1921 reflected the unfinished work of Stephen Long. One month after his death, the Sturgis Colored School was empty, save for one little girl. She was followed a couple of days later by a few more girls. Mrs. Mattie Tull, the young black teacher, had a listed enrollment of 42 registered students, but she never saw all of those students at one time. The boys didn't show up until mid-November, and by the first days of April, the Sturgis Colored School had let out for the summer.

But Stephen Long's passionate message did not die with him. The movement for a better education was a seed that, although slowly, did begin to grow.

A group of parents whose children attended schools, like Sturgis, banded together and approached the Worcester County Board of Education with a simple request – new school desks for the children. Much to the amazement of the parents, the board agreed that new desks were necessary and an order for new desks was placed. A carpenter was also hired. When the new desks arrived, they were delivered to the white schools. The carpenter was sent to fix all the used desks discarded by the white schools, and when he finished, the repaired desks were delivered to the black schools. Perhaps the Sturgis School received a few of those "new" desks.

When the school year of 1937-38 closed, the children were transferred to a new school that had been established in Pocomoke City. This new school was named the Stephen Long School, in honor of the slain educator.

Once the students were gone, Willie Sturgis, the son of the property's original owner, used the small building as his home. He put a partition in the middle of the room and even created a semi-loft in the front with a set of incredibly narrow steps. This was truly a feat given the tight quarters of the tiny structure. For heating and cooking purposes, he installed a wood stove. Willie Sturgis lived there for an unknown length of time until he became ill and moved to Baltimore, Maryland to live with family.

The years passed and the little school stood empty and abandoned in a field just off Brantley Road. Trees and vines grew up all around it; weeds and grasses grew wild where children once played. But what seemed like a dilapidated old shed on a country road was waiting to be discovered, waiting to be useful once again. It had one more life to live.

Two women banded together to save it: Annie Oliver and Carolyn Jones. Although Annie Oliver never attended the Sturgis School, she became interested in it because her siblings had gone to school there. Carolyn Jones, who lived near the school, was also president of the Worcester County Historical Society. Together, they organized a group in 1996 and decided to buy the building from the Sturgis family. Operating under the auspices of the Worcester County Historical Society, they motivated the community, pulling in every available resource – the mayor, lawyers, historical society members, citizens, and any and everyone who was interested in saving the old Sturgis School.

Photographs taken of the Sturgis One Room School in its original environment show a small, wooden building, just slightly larger than sixteen feet by twenty feet, covered in moss and weeds. A tree was growing through a portion of its eaves and the paint was peeling.

PHOTOGRAPH COURTESY OF JAMES AND SUDIE GATLING
AND THE STURGIS ONE ROOM SCHOOL MUSEUM

Another photograph shows the advocate group standing in front of the old school. Every mouth is smiling.

The town of Pocomoke donated a corner lot for the project and the country school found a new home in downtown Pocomoke in the fall of 1997. The school was a sad sight to see. It needed more than love: it needed a new foundation and a new roof as time and weather had taken a collective toll on the structural integrity of the school.

James Gatling stepped forward to become the President of the group. With James at the helm, serious restorations began, including a new roof and a new foundation. Sudie Gatling took an interest in the school and helped the group complete their application for non-profit status. The museum now operates through grants, funds from Pocomoke City and Worcester County, and donations from businesses, charities, and citizens.

Sudie and James Gatling have taken this one-room school under their collective wing. Both are retired educators who, along with a group of dedicated volunteers, organize and manage the small museum. James and the board handle the business side of things while Sudie details the history of the schoolhouse as though she lived it herself. Immediately, a visitor is pulled into the story by Sudie Gatling's voice, and by the smile on her lips and the brightness in her eyes. You cannot help it; her enthusiasm for the one-room school lights up her face. She smiles as she talks of her mannequins – the teacher and children at the front of the room. They came from Scher's, a downtown department store, but they were white mannequins. She says she took them home and reworked their features, their complexion, and dressed them in period clothing.

The task of filling the school with period artifacts proved difficult; however, the majority of the items were donated or purchased locally. There is one piece in the school that attracts Sudie's attentions and affections – an old school desk patented in 1863, the same year as Lincoln's Emancipation Proclamation. This desk and an old oak bench came to the Sturgis One Room School Museum from the remains of the Tindley School, so named after the legendary Reverend Charles Albert Tindley. Tindley was a black man born into slavery in Worcester County who went on to become well educated. He learned two languages and wrote many hymns, one of which was "I Shall Overcome." This was later adapted into the widely popular hymn "We Shall Overcome."

There are two other desks from 1881 that remind visitors of an older era, but these are a bit of an oddity. One of the most interesting aspects of the Sturgis One

Room School is that nothing in the schoolhouse is a matched set. Sudie Gatling says she prefers it that way because that is exactly how black rural schools were furnished - with hand-me-downs, one-of-a-kinds, and throw-aways. The bookshelves are filled with random schoolbooks, torn and tattered, yellowed and ripped. One book dates to 1849.

Sudie is proud of each item in the schoolhouse, whether it was found in a box at an auction house or donated from a local resident. She has memorized the fragments of information that can be traced to this tiny structure, and when she tells the story of the Sturgis One Room School, you are there.

"This is history, and I don't mind telling it," Sudie tells her visitors. Her voice is reassuring when she speaks of this history and she reminds you that much progress has been made. The Sturgis One Room School Museum exists today because a diverse community banded together to save it. The doors are open because of the generosity and cooperation of men and women of all colors and creeds. Sudie is both touched and proud of the diversity of its supporting group – this is a museum for all people.

Baltimore Md.
June 12, 1868.
Respectfully,
Copy of letter
Submit a report of his Inv—
through Secretary Delaware
Enclose letter of Maryland

District of Maryland and Delaware.
No. 17 N. Calvert Street.
Office of Supt. of Schools
Baltimore, Md., June 12th, 1868.

Captain,

I have the honor to report that I saw Mr. [Lewis] of Smyrna whose letter was sent [here] relating to an agreement between him and Mr. Furey to have the Bureau pay rent for use of School House in Smyrna. My reply was that he must settle any matter in dispute with the parties who made the promise; and that as to the future he must lay the matter in writing, before the Asst. Commissioner.

After visiting the Schools with Bvt. Brig. Gen. Brooks, I found the Annual Conference of the African M. E. Church in session. Knowing that they have ministers stationed in our District, I thought it important to meet with and address them briefly, upon "Collection of Claims," "Apprentices," and "Education Interests," which I did, on Saturday, June [—]. The Conference unanimously passed a [resolution]

DATED JUNE 12, 1868, THIS LETTER WAS SENT TO THE FREEDMAN'S BUREAU, DETAILING THE PROGRESS OF BLACK SCHOOLS ON DELMARVA. COPIED AT THE NATIONAL ARCHIVES.

In Pursuit of an Education

"When you come up as a black kid, especially around here, you sort of get used to the idea that there are certain places you can't go or things you can't do. Restaurants that we knew we couldn't go into because we knew we weren't welcome there. When my white friends would want to go to a certain place, they would have to change their minds about it because I was with them. It was the same problems, integration or not."

Charles Crippen, Jr. was born in April 1953 in the small town of Wattsville, Virginia in Accomack County. His parents, Charles and Mabel Crippen, were also born in Accomack County. His father was born on Chincoteague Island, and his mother was from Wattsville. Neither of his parents graduated from high school. Black children living on the island had one school that included grades first through seventh, and afterwards, the students like his father went to work in some manner of profession on the island. Since schools on the mainland were few and far between, his mother only went as far as the seventh grade as well.

After Charles and Mabel were married, they established their home in Wattsville, and began a family. The Crippens played many roles in the community. They owned a restaurant and Mabel offered room and board to construction workers who were working at the nearby military base. Charles worked as an oyster shucker in a shucking house on Chincoteague Island. In the mid-1950s, they began driving a school bus for black children, one of the few in Accomack County.

Because black children on Chincoteague did not have a high school on the island, the Crippens offered their help to transport the eighth graders to the black high school on the mainland of Virginia. The Accomack County Board of Education gave them a sign that they attached to their old station wagon. Officially, Accomack County had transportation for its black children living on the island. Each morning, the Crippens met a group of children on the island and drove them more than 30 miles inland so they could attend Mary N. Smith High School. In the afternoon, the station wagon-turned-school-bus picked them up and drove them back to Chincoteague Island.

By the time that Charles Jr. was able to go to school, the Crippens got a regular school bus. Charles Jr. entered the first grade in 1959 at Wattsville Elementary School, and segregation was still very much in effect.

Young Charles started his schooling in a two-room, two-story building that housed grades first through seventh, Mrs. Hattie Selby taught grades first through fourth on the first floor; upstairs, Mrs. Annie Mae Matthews instructed her fifth, sixth, and seventh graders. Most children respected – and feared – Annie Mae Matthews because she often wielded a thick wooden paddle. As Charles remembers it, "You didn't want her to spell out your name!" Subjects taught at Wattsville Elementary School included history, science, and basic arithmetic.

Charles Crippen, Jr. remembers going over to Chincoteague Island where his father worked as an oyster shucker. On the island, Charles Jr. would go door-to-door asking for donations for fundraisers. The funds collected in this manner provided the schools with extra money for fieldtrips. Once, they traveled to Jamestown, Virginia. Anything the school did was primarily self-funded through the efforts of the children and the good will of the community. The youngsters who raised the most amount of money would be crowned King and Queen at the Negro Carnival in Tasley, Virginia. It was an esteemed and coveted honor which Charles Jr. won twice in his younger years.

In 1963, Accomack County consolidated all of the black one and two room elementary school houses. This was the same year that Charles finished fifth grade. Out of the consolidation came two schools: North Accomack Elementary and South Accomack Elementary. When Wattsville Elementary School was shut down, Charles Crippen, Jr. and his classmates, were sent to their new school, North Accomack Elementary.

Once students finished the seventh grade, Charles recalls, they were then bused to T. C. Walker Middle school. The middle and high schools were located in central Accomack County so that all the black students could be bused there together. Charles and his friends attended the eighth grade at T. C. Walker.

After they finished there, they were bused to Mary N. Smith High School for the remainder of their schooling. Charles Jr. woke up early every morning to board his family's school bus and make the rounds with his parents to pick up the other children. Each morning on the way to school, the black school bus drove by two white high schools.

"We had a lot of older books, really used. They weren't ragged or anything, but they were used quite a bit. But at Mary N. Smith, we had a foreign language lab." Charles Jr. remembers Mary N. Smith as a nice school.

In Accomack County, integration had been a topic of conversation for years as each new school term unfolded, and it finally came to fruition for the school year of 1970-71. Charles Crippen was about to enter his senior year at Mary N. Smith when the news came; the black students would now attend Atlantic High School, an all-white high school.

The nervous students, black and white, proceeded into the school with anxious steps. Almost immediately, Charles noticed that Atlantic High School did not have a foreign language laboratory. The nervous tensions subsided just enough for the students to get used to their new school and new schedules. The year went surprisingly well.

"We didn't have nearly the problems the first year that they had the second and third year. Things went all right that year and I made some friends with the white kids."

During his senior year, Charles taught himself about electronics through a home-study program called the National Radio Institute. His friend, Brian Milbourne, who would later earn a law degree and become a judge in Accomack County, encouraged and helped Charles learn about technology. In 1971, Charles Crippen, Jr. received his diploma from Atlantic High School. Shortly after graduation, he married his high school sweetheart, Denise. His interest in electronics and computers steadily grew. After working for NASA for two years on radar systems, Charles Jr. followed in the steps of his entrepreneurial parents – he started his own business. Today, he owns DAC Computer Systems in Wattsville where he builds, sells, repairs, and refurbishes computers.

Charles Crippen, Jr. remembers segregation and he knows the high price some had to pay for an education. There is a story of about his father's cousin who went to unbelievable lengths for his diplomas. It is the story of William Crippen, a young boy from Chincoteague Island who took an incredible path in his desire for education.

* * * *

William Crippen walked each day from his home to the little schoolhouse for the black children of the island. He learned his lessons in a small classroom next to a large white church. The smell of seafood processing houses and the cries of seagulls intruded on the class, but William never seemed to notice. The teacher knew him well; quiet and extremely studious, William Crippen, unlike many young boys, loved school.

The seventh grade should have marked the end of William Crippen's education on Chincoteague Island. There was no further schooling, and many of the island's black folks received, at the most, a seventh grade education. But William Crippen was determined to go further with his education. He had heard of a high school for black children on the mainland. This news intrigued him, and William began devising a plan.

As the first day of the new school year arrived, William Crippen awoke in the middle of the night. He got dressed and gathered up his school things. In the darkness of pre-dawn, he walked down to the docks to catch the ferry to Franklin City on Virginia's mainland. As the ferry made its way across the Chincoteague Bay, daylight began to peek through the haze of clouds and fog. The ride took half an hour.

The ferry docked at Franklin City, Virginia. William Crippen got off and walked into town. He was able to hitch a ride to the main highway, Route 13. This was roughly a seven-mile trip. From there, William Crippen hitchhiked his way down to Tasley, Virginia in the central portion of Accomack County.

In Tasley, he attended class at Mary N. Smith High School, and in the afternoon when school let out, he walked back to the highway and thumbed his way back to Oak Hall. From there, he got another ride back to Franklin City where he boarded the ferry bound for Chincoteague Island. By sundown, William Crippen was home.

This journey, collectively more than 60 miles roundtrip, was made each day as he attended classes at the high school where he graduated in 1939.

But William Crippen still wasn't finished. There was a small Negro college in Princess Anne, Maryland that would accept him if he applied and if he could get to the school each day. William Crippen already knew that he could get there; he had been doing it for years. And so, each day of his collegiate career, he got up in the middle of the night, took the ferry, and hitchhiked all the way up to Princess Anne, a town that lay more than 30 miles to his north. He was undeterred, and in 1943, William Crippen received his college degree.

His journey was continued when William moved to Philadelphia. He enrolled at Temple University and later enlisted in the United States Navy. William Crippen was an exception to the rule. Most black students from Chincoteague Island, during his time, never got past the seventh grade as many of them went to work in oyster shucking houses and on the boats. The education of black children was a low priority for rural areas; students like William Crippen of Chincoteague Island, whose pursuits for an education outweigh any average sense of determination, are a rarity. Even William's cousin, Charles Crippen, Sr., never made it past the seventh grade.

But what Charles Crippen, Jr. remembers of segregation, he speaks of with a slow, careful drawl, as though extracting fragile files from a dusty archive. He is a good man who always, upon introduction, shakes your hand with a warm, firm grip. Charles tells his story without drama or inflection. His narration is simple and his deep eyes do not waver in the telling.

The Unstoppable

A major turning in the tide of segregation came at the close of World War II. Blacks had been sent out into the world as defenders of freedom to fight injustice and ethnic degradation. Yet, they returned home to find segregated lunch counters, below-average schools, and seats in the back of public buses. The irony was not lost on the black communities, and they took up a new fight at home. Segregation was going out.

By taking their plight to the courts and putting it in front of the public's eye, black leaders were able to put the damages of segregation in front of the white community. As a young black attorney for the NAACP, Thurgood Marshall began presenting cases before the Supreme Court in 1940 that ultimately set the precedent for the eventual end of legal segregation. Slaying the beast of segregation would come in increments, and arguably, the largest segment was the case of <u>Brown v. Board of Education</u>. The NAACP lawyers sought to prove to the Supreme Court that segregation in education was unconstitutional. Finally, the "separate but equal" slogan would be proven to be a dangerous myth in the education of all children.

Chief Justice Earl Warren agreed. "We come then to the question presented: Does segregation of children in public schools solely on the basis of race, even though the physical facilities and other 'tangible' factors may be equal, deprive the children of the minority group of equal education opportunities? We believe that it does."

The day after the Supreme Court made its ruling, Eastern Shore papers reported the landmark decision with massive, bold-type headlines. The Salisbury Times of Wicomico County ran this headline: "States Face Vast Problems After Court's Anti-Segregation Edict." That front page contained headlines from all over neighboring states – Delaware, Virginia, and West Virginia – and it contained blurbs from national and local fronts.

The news stunned the nation, and the deep South vocalized its dissent. A Mississippi senator declared, "The South will not abide nor obey this legislative decision by a political court. ... We will take whatever steps necessary to retain segregation in education."

But on the Delmarva Peninsula, the fervor was not so great. Many believed that integration would come eventually, but there was no great rush to begin redistricting, busing, or short-term planning. It was to be a lengthy and involved process.

The governor of Virginia was quoted as asking everyone in his state to have "cool heads, calm study, and sound judgment" in the wake of the most significant court decision in decades. The governor of West Virginia said that his state would "accept the decision" and do "whatever is right and proper under the decree."

Delaware state officials quickly pulled together to mull over the ramifications of this decision. They believed it would take time to integrate, but they agreed that Northern Delaware – Wilimington and New Castle County – would get it done before Southern Delaware. The reason: Kent and Sussex counties in Delaware had completely segregated communities, which meant that the integration of southern Delaware would be more difficult and time consuming.

In Maryland, a Worcester County school official said he did not anticipate any immediate changes, "when and if one came." The school superintendent for Wicomico County said he would review the decision and comply with it in an orderly fashion.

Although the rules had changed with the Supreme Court's decision, the implementation was going to take years, especially in the more remote and rural sections of America. The Delmarva Peninsula was just such a place. Local governments knew that full integration was years down the road, and no one seemed to be in a hurry to travel that great distance quickly.

By 1961, eight out of nine counties on the Eastern Shore of Maryland did not have any black students mixed with the white students. Officials stated that no black students had applied to the new order. In

Wicomico County, the black teenagers attended the all-black Salisbury High School while the whites attended Wicomico High School. The young children attended schools scattered all over the county – races separated.

In those early days of the 1960s, Melvin and Clara Harris, a young black couple from West Virginia, were hired as teachers in Wicomico County. Melvin Harris was a young, light-skinned black man with a deep passion for music and a sense of humor that could crack a statue. Yet underneath his jovial disposition was a backbone of iron – Melvin Harris was nobody's fool. That is except for his beautiful young wife, Clara Harris. Even at a young age, Clara had the kind of grace only found in older women who were raised on the legacy of womanhood. Together, they would have a profound effect on the youth of the county.

Because Melvin was a band director, he found himself being recruited by Royd Mahaffey, the Superintendent of Schools. Band directors were in short supply, and Melvin Harris Jr. was desperately wanted by Wicomico County; however, Melvin would not accept a position if a job wasn't available for his wife. Within days, an elementary school teaching position was found for Clara, and the Harrises moved to the Eastern Shore of Maryland.

Mahaffey told Melvin Harris when he hired him that the band situation in the county was pitiful, and not to pattern himself on the existing practices. Melvin looked him straight in the eyes and said, "I have my own style."

It would have been impossible for Mr. Royd Mahaffey to know just how true those words would prove to be.

The first year of teaching for both Melvin and Clara Harris was 1961. Melvin was teaching band at the all-black Salisbury High and Clara was at a small, all-black elementary school in Salisbury. Early in the year, Melvin noticed that the black students who were coming to him at the middle and high school level did not have a basic foundation in music education. Yet he saw that the white elementary school children were learning about music. So Melvin went to the school board and asked why the black children were not learning music education at the elementary level.

The response: no one wanted the job.

Melvin quickly answered, "I do."

He began traveling three days a week to each of the three black elementary schools in addition to the middle and high schools. He was doing the job of five band directors, and recognizing his efforts, the school board paid him fifteen cents per mile.

But then Melvin realized another crucial difference. The instruments at the all-black high school looked as though they might have been relics of the Civil War, and Melvin noticed that elementary school-aged children in the white schools were toting around shiny new trumpets and flutes. So, when his principal asked him for a list of things that he needed, Melvin's budget included new instruments for the black high school. The principal later came to Melvin and told him that he'd have to significantly cut the list, saying, "It'll look better if we don't ask for so much." And Melvin did not get the new instruments.

The following school year, Melvin made his list and instead of taking it to his principal, Melvin took it straight to the school board. The principal of the black high school nearly fainted when he saw a large moving truck pull up to the school, delivering brand new instruments to Melvin Harris. That happened during the same school year that Wicomico County made an unprecedented move: the county redistricted to bring all students together. This was the first time a geographical move towards integration had been made on the lower shore.

One of the first steps towards making this happen was sending black teachers into white schools, and even sending some white teachers into the black schools. Clara Harris had a close friend who was sent to an all white school. Prior to the first day of teaching, the black teachers who were going to the white schools had to attend a faculty meeting. In that meeting, they were given a list of what to do and, more specifically, what not to do.

Soon after, Clara was sent to teach at North Salisbury Elementary, which meant that her oldest daughter, Denise, could ride with her and go to school there. When Denise Harris took her seat in the class, she was the only black child in the room. Then the inevitable came: young Denise came home from school and wanted to know what a "nigger" was.

Clara Harris had to look her child in the eyes and explain a word that was never used in their home.

Black parents on the Eastern Shore were often upset with the way integration disrupted the lives of black students. Integration, they argued, meant that their children were forced into white schools and never the other way around. White children did not enter into previously all-black schools. The underlying reason: black schools were not as good as the white schools. Over the years, the best supplies, materials, and equipment were given to white schools, not black. While at North Salisbury, Clara Harris marveled at the recent copyright dates in her textbooks. The ones she had used at the black school were many years older.

Before the presidential election of 1968, a rumor struck Salisbury that created such a buzz about the town that it could not be ignored. Presidential candidate George Wallace, who was running on a strict anti-desegregation platform, was coming to town. The principal of the black high school approached Melvin Harris and asked if his band would go to the county airport and play for Wallace's arrival.

Melvin refused.

The principal insisted, saying again that it would look good for the band to be there. But that would not sway Melvin Harris who, on the spot, declared that he would rather give up his job than to take his kids to play for George Wallace. Simply, it was not going to happen. Melvin then suggested that the white band at Wicomico High School be asked to play for George Wallace's airport arrival.

The Wicomico High band refused to play as well.

In Clara Harris's classroom, the second graders were talking about who they would vote for in the upcoming presidential election. Many of the white children said they would vote for George Wallace, naturally repeating what their parents had said. One little boy raised his hand, and told Clara he knew the reason why the white children would vote for Wallace.

"And why is that?" Clara couldn't help herself.

"Cause he wants to send all the black kids back to the other school, and you better watch out cause you're almost!"

Clara Harris, who is a light-skinned black woman, bit her lip to keep from laughing as she walked into the closet room to compose herself. Clara Harris understood the innocence of children.

For the teachers, integration was a source of confusion and pitfalls. Because children and teachers of different races had never met in a classroom before, problems arose frequently. White teachers referred to the "black skin" and "kinky hair" of their students; black children rebelled against the new white authority figures. The misunderstanding was a deep dividing line, and building a bridge to cover the distance would take years of integration and familiarization.

Even amongst themselves, the black teachers had questions. By whom should they sit at faculty meetings? Did they sit next to the white teachers? Were they expected to sit with other black teachers? Or could they just sit with their friends, regardless of skin color?

The black teachers could tell that the community was emotionally split on integration. While the students seemed to handle it fine, their parents often showed a sense of resentment at having a black person teach their child. No one said anything to Melvin or Clara Harris, but it wasn't about words. It was the feeling they got looking into the eyes of a parent. Everyone knew.

As integration progressed, the intensity settled down and more and more children became accustomed to seeing all races in the classroom as both teacher and student. Full integration of Wicomico County schools was marked in 1974, twenty long years after <u>Brown v. Board of Education</u>. Melvin and Clara Harris saw the entire process, and have retired from education in Wicomico County.

"Our children suffered." Clara says that there were two main effects of integration on the young black children: it made them competitive or it made them apathetic. The children, she says, either wanted to beat the white children by earning better grades or higher scores, or, they decided not to even bother with trying in the classroom. And as she says this, there is a distinct sound of sadness in her voice.

Time passed and the dividing line became less and less visible. The children in Clara Harris's classroom – especially the young girls – idolized Clara as she was tall, slender, and beautiful. Little girls marveled at her high heels and wondered how long she must have practiced to conquer them. Clara Harris was a lady and earned respect through her simple grace.

Melvin Harris is probably the most beloved educator in the history of Wicomico County. His students – all races – adored him, and this unending adoration was often the spur in the saddle of many of his colleagues. Melvin said that most of his problems with other faculty members stemmed more from his popularity among the students than from his skin color. He was the only black band director Wicomico County had after integration and the only one since, but that is not what he should be remembered for, and he would agree. Throughout his teaching career, which lasted more than thirty years, Melvin Harris established himself as a first-rate musician, teacher, and mentor.

"Yes, I remember segregation." But Melvin Harris is quick to point out that children today have different experiences. It is not the same for them.

And he is right. Eventually, everything changes and what we once knew as absolute truths either get lost along the way or evolve into something new and different. We are creatures of adaptation – our minds and hearts change. This is unstoppable.

However it may have occurred in the different counties on the Delmarva Peninsula, integration has dug its roots deep into the soil of our region at long last. Opposition existed; opposition was overcome. The code of normalcy is different with each generation, and hopefully, the educational system will continue to improve and the products of that system, the children, will continue to grow together, in and out of the classroom.

The Adriatic Sea

ANA'S STORY

The green ocean waves roll onto a sandy shore. Local folks bask on towels, laughing in the sun while children play in the breakers. They squeal as the foam races over their toes. Sea birds squawk overhead, casually dipping into the water to snatch a fish. A couple of teenagers have set up a little picnic nearby; they steal sweet glances at each other.

Boats line the marina. They are marked by scars of rust and warts of barnacles. Rope nets dry in the sun.

Nearby there are seafood markets where people can buy the catch of the day.

The beach is lively place; no one could imagine a more beautiful or relaxing place under the wide blue sky. Time passes slowly. The ocean keeps breaking.

This is not the Atlantic. It is the Adriatic. But they share more in common than what meets the American eye.

*   *   *

Ante Lipic came home from work unusually late. He looked exhausted; his eyes were red and the tan that graced the curves of his face was reduced to a white pallor. Merima did not notice him immediately and spoke curtly with him. Her dinner was growing cold and the children, Ana and Tomislav, had already started eating.

"I have something to tell you, Merima." Ante felt a pain in his chest.

"Not now. Dinner is getting cold."

Ante said nothing and dropped into his chair at the head of the table. His beautiful blonde children smiled at him, "Ciao, tata! How were the people at the store?" Ante owned a local merchant store in Tuzla, Bosnia. They had just moved there within the last year and a half.

"Fine. Just fine." Ante's voice trailed off and he could not look at his children, not with the news he was about to share with his family. Their eyes, he thought, so wide and clear. He was not a tall man, but the unseen weight on his shoulders pushed him down, nearly equal with the table. The nightmare was beginning.

Merima sat down and the family said grace.

"I have something to tell you." He tried again.

"What?"

"At the store today, Petar told me that the Serbians are going to shut down Bosnia."

Ana and Tomislav stopped eating. Merima stared at her husband. The children looked from their mother to their father and back again.

"Ante, don't say such things in front of the children."

"It's true," he said.

"But how?"

He explained what he had been told by his Serbian friend. The government of Serbia had issued a warning to all Serbs living in Bosnia to get out before three o'clock the next day. Otherwise, they would be trapped.

"Trapped? Ante, you're scaring me."

"The Serbians will take over Bosnia, Tuzla, everything tomorrow. We will all be prisoners."

Ana looked at her brother across the table. They went to school every day and played games in the streets. How would they be trapped? Her stomach wound itself in a knot around the little portion of fish and rice she had just eaten. She did not understand how little children could become prisoners, and she did not know that the worst was yet to come and that the long struggle of survival was just beginning.

* * *

Ana and I could no longer deny the truth – autumn was upon us. The trees that lined the sidewalk to our apartment had already begun the ritual, trading their supple greenery for nakedness under heavy clouds. The October twilight came earlier every day. There would be no escape without facing more days and months of colder weather, and November was just around the corner. Spring, we concluded, comes at a price.

"I hate cold weather. I've never gotten used to it," Ana said.

"But you've lived here for the past six years."

"I know, and I've still never gotten used to it."

Ana's parents had come to visit us for the weekend and we were in a hurry to get back in time for dinner. They were staying at a local motel since our apartment was so small; couches and floors are no place for parents.

We exchanged grimaces as we hurried down the sidewalk. We were unhappy with the cold wind in our faces. I asked Ana if she thought our heater would hold up for the winter months. She doubted it, but we decided to hope anyway.

She and I were roommates at Washington College, a small liberal arts school in Chestertown, Maryland. I met Ana when she came to visit the school as a potential transfer student and we became instant friends because it is impossible to dislike her. She transferred to Washington College before the start of our junior year and, from that moment forward, we were nearly inseparable.

When we reached our little bungalow, I opened the door and was greeted with the smell of fresh trout frying on our stove and the distinct sound of Croatian conversation.

Earlier that morning, her parents had gone downtown to the open seafood market. Merima Lipic enjoyed going downtown to look at the fish because it reminded her of the seafood markets in Croatia. She bought ten pounds of various fish to take back home. They lived in Harrisburg, Pennsylvania. Ana's parents spent the whole morning touring Chestertown and admiring its historic beauty. Afterwards, Ante Lipic went to the liquor store and bought a two-gallon jug of white table wine for that evening's dinner.

As we entered, "Hellos" and "Ciaos" were exchanged and Merima kissed us both. Being kissed on both cheeks is an awkward thing for Americans, especially those from the country. But with Merima Lipic, I enjoyed her custom and her smiling nature.

"Stephanie, do you eat the fish?" she asked. Her green eyes searched mine under the fluorescent overhead bulbs. Ana also confused her articles and often asked me to read over her school reports to make sure she had properly used "a" "an" and "the." In the Croatian language, articles don't exist.

I smiled, "Yes, thank you."

"Ante, get them some wine." Ante was riveted to the television because there was an international soccer game being broadcast from Spain. He headed for his jug of wine. "This," he stated as he eased the jug to the counter, "is how we drink in our country." Ante had a gentle smile that rested on a wide, tanned face. He was the kind of man that everyone smiled at, and Merima, especially, returned his grins. Ante took a glass and repositioned himself on the sofa, his attention falling back to the game.

After pouring a glass of wine and dropping into a chair, I closed my eyes and envisioned myself in the Balkan country. All around me, lemon trees and purple vineyards blossomed in the warm air. Everything was framed by shades of gold or green or faded blue. The smell of olives and the rushing pulse of the sea filled the air. I saw village homes, nestled closely together like they had been friends all along the decades of their existence. An afternoon sun spilled through slender rectangular windows, casting golden highlights on tiled floors and cracked walls. I pretended I could see it all. I wished my little apartment had flowers growing wildly and purposefully by the front steps, and I wished worn pottery rested in the cupboards.

Fish crackled and rice boiled on the stove as Merima took command of our small kitchen while Ante drank his wine and cursed the soccer officials on the television. Ana and her mother conversed in their native tongue and I pretended I could understand. I wanted to get lost in something I did not know.

There was something between this family. A deep connection bonded them in a way I knew I would never understand. Ana and her family survived the war that ravaged the Balkans. When Bosnia-Herzegovnia asserted its independence, it incurred the wrath of Serbia, led by the brutal Slobodan Milosevic. The horrific Bosnian War claimed thousands of lives and all but destroyed the once beautiful region of Yugoslavia.

Ana saw it all.

* * *

Ana was born in Tuzla, Bosnia in late May 1979. Shortly after her birth, the family moved to Split, a major coastal city in Croatia where she spent most of her childhood years. Merima Lipic held a law degree and was a ballerina until she was 25 and became pregnant with Ana. Ante Lipic owned several merchant stores. Their home was forty feet from the beaches of the Adriatic Sea. Tomislav, her little brother, was born two years after Ana and the pair was inseparable from the first moments of hide-and-seek. The neighborhood was full of young children who played games until their parents called them in for supper.

For years, the two spoke in a secret language. Tomislav had a lisp that made his "s's" sound like "ssh's", but Ana always understood and was very patient when he spoke. She never laughed at his tongue's misbehavior. They would sit at the dinner table and converse in words of gibberish while Merima and Ante stared at each other. Tomislav was quiet and dreamed of being a famous pianist while Ana decided she would one day become a doctor and cure all kinds of ailments.

Photographs of the young Lipic children bear great similarities – sun-kissed skin, blonde hair, green eyes full of eagerness and innocence. For the first five years of his life, Ana was the only person Tomislav would talk to. Merima hardly ever got a direct word from her son. Although she was the older sibling, Ana needed Tomislav with her all the time. They shared the same room until she was 11 years old because Ana could not sleep by herself. Nothing seemed right if he wasn't close by. And just as the sea cannot pull itself away from the coast, Ana and Tomislav never parted company. Even though Tomislav wore thick glasses and stumbled when he walked, Ana held his hand as they made their way down through the cliffs to explore the caves within. She never let go, not even when she wanted to run and see the insides of the caverns first. No, she held onto his hand and showed him the best places to put his feet; she showed him where ancient sea monsters and devilish pirates most likely hid their treasures. And as always, Tomislav, with wide eyes and a thin, wet smile, was quiet and faithful.

The Lipic family moved to Bosnia in 1990 because her father had purchased a store in Tuzla. There, her mother began working as a tax collector. Life was prosperous. The Lipic family still had their home by the shore in Split, Croatia and another apartment on the small island of Hvar in the Adriatic, which lies just off the southern coast of Split. For a time, everything was peaceful.

* * *

The smell of the cooking trout created chaos in my stomach. Merima had ordered Ana out of the kitchen because "she was no good cook." I smiled because I know my friend is not, as she puts it, "domestic."

"Oh no! That was penalty! That was penalty!" cried Ante. Ana told me that her father played on a men's league in Harrisburg and even refereed a few games. For an older man, Ante was in astoundingly good shape. Barrel-chested and no taller than five feet five inches, he moved like a cannonball that is always on target.

Ante loved two things: his family and European football. His father was a great football player in Yugoslavia and there was a Lipic family legend that he was honored by the Yugoslavian team with an honorary Olympic silver medal. Ana remembers being captivated by the medal that sat on the mantel in his house. All his life, Ante was running and kicking, every movement simulated to emulate a legendary father who was constantly described in heroic details. But Ante had inherited something greater than athletic ability and a dominating presence from his father – he owned himself like no other person I had ever met before. Immediately, I respected him because he almost single-handedly saved his family from certain death, and in saving Ana's life, I will always be grateful. During a commercial, he explained to me that American football is not like his football because his was "played with the grace". When the game came back on, Ante slipped back into focus.

I looked outside and saw the bare tree branches. "It's beginning to get really cold outside," I said.

Ana replied, "Back home it never got this cold."

"Ana is right," called Merima from the kitchen. "Croatia is very warm all the year."

"See, we're right near Italy. Actually, as a kid growing up, I could stand on my front doorstep and see the lighthouse on the Croatian island of Solta which is out in the Adriatic Sea."

"Komiza too, Ana." Ante turned his attention momentarily from the soccer game on our television to remind his daughter of another island's lighthouse.

"Come, dinner is ready," commanded Merima, with a broad smile.

The Lipic family and I took our places around our small dinner table – fried fish with lemon over rice with white wine and crusty bread. Merima smiled and nodded at us. Looking across the room at her husband, she frowned, "Ante! Come!"

A final curse and he was seated.

*   *   *

The decision was made at the dinner table. Ana and her brother would be packed up and sent to Croatia while Merima and Ante remained in Bosnia until it was safe for them to come back. They couldn't leave their home and jobs; after all, how does a family quit their life in twenty-four hours? Jobs, friends, home – everything was to be erased in minutes as Serbia vowed to keep its promise.

"It may be nothing," Ante tried to assure his family. "We cannot lose everything here."

Merima resigned herself to her husband's hopeful opinion, but her instinct said something else. What if the Serbians could truly take everything away? Her eyes fell upon her children: who would she be without them? "Ana, take Tomislav upstairs and go pack. Make sure you get everything you may need."

Tomislav stared at his sister, looking for direction. Ana was quiet. Merima looked at the plate in front of her, and she began to cry.

"You heard your mother, Ana. We'll be up soon to help you."

Ana slid down from the table and took her small brother by the hand. As they slowly stepped up the stairs, Tomislav asked, "Ana, what'ssh happening?"

"We have to go away. Some soldiers are coming to live here."

Tomislav froze on the stairs. "Where are we going to go?"

"Home, back to Croatia, to stay with Aunt Mili and Aunt Gracija."

"What about Mami and Tata?"

"They will stay here."

"With the ssholdierssh?" Tears spilled over his eyes; he never blinked.

"I don't know, Tomislav. Come on."

The Lipic children packed their brown suitcases. Their parents drove them to the train station a few hours later.

"I love you, my babies." Merima pulled both children close to her. Ante touched their blonde heads. This was to be the last time they saw Ana and Tomislav for nearly a year. By 3 o'clock in the afternoon on May 15, 1992, Merima and Ante Lipic were prisoners of Tuzla.

Ana was sent to live with an aunt in Split, and Tomislav was sent to live with another aunt who had two boys of her own. Neither aunt could care for both of the children. Ana and Tomislav were able to communicate with each other a few times, but they had no contact with their parents for almost an entire year. The Serbian fragmentation was complete. Each night, she crawled into a single bed in a room without Tomislav. His absence was a constant, physical pain. Facing the wall with her thighs pressed against her ribs, she closed her eyes and prayed for her family to be safe and that she might see them again. She feared if she forgot to say her prayer even one night, then they would die the next day. This simple prayer became her only link to her family and she had to do her part to keep them safe.

For a 12 year-old girl alone in war, hope and fear occupy the same spaces.

Ana had continued going to school in Croatia and for almost a year, she had not communicated with her family. Contact was made finally through satellites that had been linked up over the three warring countries of Serbia, Croatia, and Bosnia. Her father and mother wept at the recognition of their children's voices. Ana and Tomislav begged to come home and be with their parents, even if that meant leaving the safety of sunny, southern Croatia and sneaking into hostile territory. Ante agreed because he could no longer endure the separation of his family, and so he smuggled himself out of Tuzla on a Sunday morning in April of 1993.

When Ante got to Ana and Tomislav, they almost did not recognize him. He had lost many pounds and his eyes were sunken and dull. That he had once been so full of vibrant energy and thick with muscle was almost unbelievable. Ana and Tomislav paused for a brief second. Could this ragged man in front of them be the father who, in their minds, could eat all the fish in the Adriatic? Could it be the son of their Herculean grandfather? Later, they would learn that there was little food in Tuzla, Bosnia. Normally, the trip from Croatia to Bosnia would take six hours, but Serbian forces had bombed all the major roadways. The only way back to Tuzla was through the high, blizzard-encrusted Dinaric Alps on secret buses.

Ante was able to get himself and his children on a bus that same Sunday night. The tickets cost an absurd amount of money, but they had no choice because Merima was still in Bosnia. Fifty passengers loaded onto the bus. There were six children total: a baby in the back of the bus with its young mother, three small children in the front, and Ana and her little brother. Half of the group was elderly and the other half was middle-aged; many of them were searching for a way to get back to their families. There were few women on the bus because, typically, only men were allowed to make the dangerous trip into Bosnia. The bus had to travel over three different territories occupied by three separate and warring forces: Muslim, Serbian, and Croatian. If either of the forces captured the bus, then some of the passengers could be killed. There were members of each nation riding on that secret bus. Ana and her brother wedged themselves between the window and their father. The nervous journey into the mountains began.

Ana rode through villages she had never seen and mountain passages she had never heard of. Sometimes she would notice that the bus was not even traveling on a road but a small path cut between slices of snow and rock. At the end of the first day, a blizzard descended upon the mountain passage. Four feet of snow fell in what seemed like seconds, forcing the secret bus to Bosnia off the road.

The driver slowed the bus, "I cannot go any further! The storm is too bad! We must stop."

"You cannot stop. Please, you must try to keep going!" pleaded one old Muslim man.

Other passengers begged too, but everyone knew the storm was too much for the bus. The driver feared the most: he knew the bus's limitations and those limits had just about been reached. "The snow is too bad. We must wait and see if the weather clears. I'm sorry, please, I'm sorry."

And the bus stopped moving.

They could not deny their fate; death haunted the passengers through a white veil of snow pressed against the frosted windows. The bus was almost dead in the small mountain passage; nightfall could not obscure the flashes of white from the storm.

"I can keep the bus running for a short time to keep us warm," the bus driver told his passengers. Responsibility weighed down awfully upon him. He kept the bus running as the blizzard raged on, but the effort could not last. "I'm sorry. I'm so sorry." And then he prayed.

Ante pulled Ana and Tomislav close to him. "Everything is going to be all right. Help will come soon," he told them. "Help will be here soon."

During the night, the battery weakened and the passengers listened intensely as the low hum of the battery rose and fell, revived and dropped, and then finally died. They waited, but the silence overwhelmed them. As though the surrounding cold had frozen the air inside the bus, the stillness pressed hard on their ears and the fifty passengers slowly began to freeze. The nearest village was 25 miles away. And so they waited and waited inside the bus that was being buried by the blizzard. Help did not come.

With each passing moment, the passengers were panicking more and more – the fear of being buried alive pushed many to the edges of their seats and others to the edges of their minds. Tempers flared at the bus driver who hung his head as he sunk back into his seat. The young mother in the back of the bus asked for blankets or coats to wrap around her child. Some of the passengers offered their own coats to wrap around the little baby. And like this, they waited for the morning.

Once daylight appeared to break, six men on the bus, including Ante, decided that they would go search for help. They decided to go back to the last village – it was the only chance they had for survival. The passengers piled their extra clothes on the men for protection against the freezing temperatures. As Ante kissed his children, their cold noses and stiff, dry lips pressed against his unshaven cheeks. They felt like corpses and their open green eyes intensified his horror. Only their blinking kept him rooted in the living. "Stay here. You'll be safe. Don't worry, Tata will be back soon." And then he disappeared into the snow.

Ana and Tomislav wrapped their arms around each other, clinging to one another for warmth and support. They were all they had left.

The passengers waited and the snow continued to fall. The young mother in the back of the bus sang a lullaby to her baby and clutched the small bundle close to her chest. "Hush, hush, my little angel," the young woman sang. "All around you, dreams are being woven." And for several hours, there was nothing but fear and cold, snow and themselves, and the songs of the young mother.

The six men walked directionless in the snow. They dropped an article of clothing every few minutes to help them find their way back. They moved forward and then backwards, side to side, and in circles. Fragments of ice hurled by the high winds scratched their faces; the freezing temperatures numbed them to the marrow of their bones. As they roamed, blinded by the blizzard, UN soldiers from Manchester, England spotted them. The soldiers took them into custody and transported them to the UN sub-station. Once inside, the soldiers looked for a translator.

The commander of the base stepped forward and asked his troops, "Does anyone know their language?"

Ante, in his younger years, was a sailor and he remembered a little of the English he picked up on the ships.

"Excuse," he began. The commander turned to him. "Child, woman, ah, help, ah, bus, stop." Ante pointed to the door, stammering and searching for words to convey his message.

"There are children out there?"

"Yes, yes! Bus!"

The commander stepped forward and spoke slowly and carefully to Ante. "Can you," he pointed his finger to him, "show us," he pointed to himself, "where the bus is?" he pointed to the door.

"Yes, help!"

The commander understood well enough: a bus with women and children on it was trapped in the storm. He turned to his men, a rescue mission was put into effect. The soldiers were dispersed into their proper places. The men with Ante looked hopeful but confused. Ante explained to them that the commander now knew about the bus, about the people on board.

More than 100 soldiers were deployed in tanks and armored trucks to recover the bus. Because of the storm, the UN soldiers could not use helicopters. In a matter of hours, the convoy came upon the half-covered bus. When the soldiers entered the bus, they witnessed a nightmare. Many passengers had developed frostbite on their faces and hands. The baby in the back of the bus was dead in its mother's arms.

The soldiers, dressed in heavy snow gear, told the group that the children and the elderly would be moved first, moving two at a time. The passengers were nearly frozen; their arms were not mobile enough to hold the edges of the blankets around themselves. To get the people from the bus and into the tanks and armored trucks, the soldiers tightly wrapped them like skinny mummies in thick blankets. When all the passengers were loaded, the soldiers looked at them. The passengers were in awful condition; their fingers would not bend and their eyes would not cry. The silence enunciated the suffering. A UN British commander gave an order to move and the refugees were taken to the substation.

They were taken to a large room that looked like an empty warehouse or a large cargo hanger. The elderly and the five remaining children were given cots to sleep on, but there were not enough for everyone. Several men slept on the concrete floor. Ante slept on two chairs that he pushed together. The storm raged on, but the base was warm. There, the refugees finally slept.

In the food lines, the English cook tried to teach Ana and Tomislav a few words of English.

"Soup." He pointed to the chicken noodle bin.

Ana and Tomislav looked at one another and shrugged.

"Soup." The cook picked up a ladle and poured out the contents, "Soup."

"Soup?" Ana repeated.

"Sschoup." Tomislav's lisp amused the men.

"Good, good." He patted their heads and gave them extra crackers. The Lipic children knew an English word.

The soldiers invited the children to watch movies with them, mostly American movies. Ana and Tomislav, who knew only one English word, stared at the television screen. They picked up a few more American words, the very kind that their parents wished they hadn't.

In a few days, the base, which had become a haven, was running low on water, food, and other supplies. After the fourth day, the soldiers made an attempt to dig out the bus and they were successful. The UN soldiers worked for six long hours to drag it up the mountain. With the bus refueled, the thankful passengers were soon on their nervous way again.

The day after Ante left, Merima Lipic was able to make contact with her family in Croatia. The family members told her that he had arrived and had already left with the children. Everyone thought them dead, and in that one day, Merima's beautiful blonde hair turned completely white. Merima was alone, a prisoner in a war-torn country with no husband and no children. Thursday came and Ante showed up with Ana and

Tomislav in hand. After almost a year, Merima hugged and kissed her children.

*   *   *

The fried trout smothered in tartar sauce and buttered white rice hit my stomach just right. Merima explained to me that fish and other seafood are the major source of food where they lived in Croatia.

"We get the fresh fish every morning," she said. "And I cook it at every dinner."

Ante added, "We have our own grapes so we make the wine ourself."

"But this is not tradition here," Merima said. Most American families go out to big restaurants to eat dinner, she explained. I agreed with her mostly, but I was quick to defend my mother's home cooking.

"My mother cooks dinner every night."

"From the 'scratch'?"

Merima had a point. Is buying a package of beef from the grocery case and then baking it in the oven considered "scratch"? Is putting tea bags in the Mr. Coffee Ice Tea Maker considered "scratch"? I was quite sure that Mrs. Smith's apple pies were not scratch, but my mother never used those kind anyway.

"Well," I said. "She does not always go to the butcher for meat, but she does cook it on her own. She cooks on the stove and bakes in the oven, not in the microwave." I had no idea if I was making myself clear, but I enunciated, tried to lose my lower Maryland country accent, and used my hands as much as possible.

"With the spices and sauce?"

"Yes, exactly." Merima understood me fine.

"Are the potatoes mashed in a box?"

I hesitated. "Sometimes, but my grandmother always uses real potatoes."

Merima beamed at me. "That's how we do it, too."

I remembered how my mother has memorized countless recipes and can pull them from memory with such simple ease. She rarely used a measuring cup; her hands are instinctive in the kitchen. I recalled how my grandmother fixed every meal from a base of flour, Crisco, sugar, and eggs. She cooked as though a hundred men were coming to eat at her table and she never threw away a single scrap of food. My grandfather would go out on the water and harvest clams and oysters to bring home to his family. This was how Merima Lipic loved to cook – fresh and by her hands.

The similarity struck me. Languages, oceans, and continents apart, there are commonalties between the Eastern Shore life and the Adriatic life. We work the water and eat what we take, just as they do. We would not know what to do without our seafood just as they would not. In Croatia, they grow their own fruits and vegetables; on the Eastern Shore, farmers are as important as the sun itself. The thought that my Maryland, my Eastern Shore could be like Ana's Croatia made me feel welcome in a place I had never seen. Food may be universal, but the care that Merima Lipic and the women in my family take with it was a natural bridge between our cultures. I was happy to have a belly full of such cooking.

As we ate, I noticed the striking resemblance between mother and daughter. Both women had amazing, light green eyes set deep into olive skin, blonde hair drawn back into careless buns. I was reminded of photographs of my mother as a young woman – we could be twins living in two different times. The passing of physical looks is easy to trace, but what is more difficult to place is the passing of grace, of strength, of determination. What makes Ana strong comes from Merima; what gives me courage comes from my mother.

I see in Ana those intangibles. There is something deeper than the crossing of an ocean and stronger than its tides in Ana. She has eyes that refuse to let their appraiser forget her.

She has eyes that will not forget.

*   *   *

Tuzla bomb shelters had two identities. By day, they were schools and gyms for the local children; by night, they were harbors from the threatening Serbian skies. Ana and Tomislav's school was also their closest bomb shelter. After school, the children would play basketball games. Ana, a point-guard, ran circles around her opponents. Before dark, the children dispersed to their respective neighborhoods.

At night, Ana and Tomislav lay awake straining their ears toward the ceiling. She was afraid to breathe sometimes, fearing her breath would be enough to stir up the sky. Tomislav lay awake in the bed next to her. If the night was silent, they would slip into sleep without thinking. If not, there would be no sleep for days. Serbian attacks on Tuzla were frequent. But for small children, even one attack is too many.

Ana and Tomislav had only been home a few days when they witnessed their first Serbian air strike. A bomb struck. The apartment building shook. Ana's eyes flew open. The children cried out for one another. Another bomb struck closer.

"Ana! Tomislav! Get under the desk, now! Hurry!" Ante yelled to his children. The building shook again.

Merima screamed and cried out for her children, "Get under something! Hide!"

The two Lipic children slid under the desk against the wall opposite of the window. Flashes of light blinded their green eyes. The children listened to their mother screaming and sobbing down the hallway.

"Mami, we're under the desk! We're all right!"

All night bombs dropped and lights flashed, sirens blew and people screamed. Ana and Tomislav watched the skies light up and held their hands over their ears.

The next morning, there was no school. Bomb threats, warning sirens, and lit night skies became part of their lives; they adjusted their routine to the scent in the air. Every night that the bombs fell, Ana feared her ceiling would crash down on top of her family and no one would find them alive. How long will our building stand against the shaking, she wondered?

As the war continued, the Lipic family desperately needed food but there was little means to buy it. Money was of no value – the only available option was to trade with farmers outside of the city. They were among those who had what little food remained in the imprisoned country.

One afternoon, Ante drove the family car, a Renault, to a farm close to the city. Back and forth, Ante and the farmer negotiated, and finally struck a deal. The farmer took the car and Ante took two bags of flour. Merima stretched the two bags into a month and a half's worth of food for her family. Ana now understood why her father was so skinny when he came back to Croatia to get her and her brother. Ana and little Tomislav were also growing smaller.

There was a shortage of medical supplies as well. Merima's mother was a diabetic, and once the war began, shipments of insulin all but stopped. She received intermittent shots, which came less and less frequently, and her condition deteriorated rapidly. After a short time, Serbia cut off all medical supply shipments. Within days, she was dead.

Ana remembers the day the women from the Bosnian concentration camps came to Tuzla. The University near her home was turned into a housing compound run by a nearby Muslim mosque. Every day, psychologists from Tuzla dealt with the Bosnian and Croatian victims – they were of every age, young girls to elderly women. Nearly every woman had been raped, and if once, then many times. Mothers watched their daughters taken by the same soldier who had just violated them. Sisters were taken and grandmothers too. Hundreds of women carried smaller Serbian soldiers in their bellies as they walked the perimeter of their new prison. Suicide stalked the University, through what remained of the women. Ana remembers their faces, their swollen bellies; she remembers her father and mother telling her not to look and telling her there was no story to tell. But the young girls at the bomb shelter talked and they told Ana what the soldiers had done. No one could save them now, she thought, no one.

The next loss suffered by the Lipic family was the day the Serbians cut off the electric to all the apartment complexes in Tuzla. Without electricity, there was no water, no heat, no air conditioning, no lights, and no telephone. Bringing water into the apartment involved dragging buckets of water up sixteen flights of stairs to their eighth-floor home. An older couple, who lived below them on the seventh-floor, showed Merima and Ante how to make candles. Take a glass, they said, fill it with cooking oil and a little water. Then drop a shoelace in it. So, every night, Ante and Merima would light their shoelace candles to eat dinner and tell stories to their children.

Relief aid from the UN brought foodstuffs like flour, oil, butter, milk, and sometimes sugar. The women in the apartment complex all came together a few times a day to discuss what they were feeding their families. With so few options, variety often lacked. If

Merima needed flour for a meal, she could often trade some oil or sugar with one of the women in her building. Since there was no electric to run the refrigerators, the women stored milk in tight containers outside on their balconies for a few days. Then, in gas stoves, they baked the jars; this produced edible cheese for the families, which lasted longer than the milk ever would have.

The women were resourceful, and the families depended on their mothers and wives to help them eat and live. A single loaf of bread was stretched to feed four for an entire day: a thin slice for breakfast, another for lunch, and then the rest was eaten for dinner. Many times, Merima offered up her portion to her children because their shallow bellies ate at her more than her own hunger.

To make shampoo, Merima and the others picked chamomile and other fragrant grasses from behind the complex, cooked them on the stove and added some oil. For soap, oil and fat excess or butter was cooked together and cooled, the resulting chunks where sliced in small strips and everyone was reminded to use it sparingly. The electricity would come and go, and the families would have to wait for it to come on before flushing the toilets. Sometimes they'd have to wait for an hour and sometimes they waited for five days. Pages from cookbooks, magazines, and books were torn out and used for toilet paper. One day, Ante called out to his family, "Anyone care to save Tolstoy?"

No one did, and "War and Peace" became toilet paper.

Merima picked the other women's' brains to get ideas on what to feed her family. Strange gruels borne of flour and other ingredients tried to quiet growling stomachs. One night, there was dandelion salad. But for all Merima's ingenious and creative efforts, Ana was growing thinner and weaker. Soon, she was so weak that she had great difficulty climbing the stairs to the apartment.

*   *   *

We insisted that Merima leave the dishes on the table, "You cook, we clean."

She doubled kissed Ana and me and then went to sit with her husband. Ante had gone back to the soccer game. He was just in time for the final few minutes.

"Mr. Lipic, who won?" I asked.

He shrugged. "It is no matter. Both teams play bad ball, very poor. I no like that in football game."

Ana rolled her eyes at me and we cleared the table quickly. Merima and Ante decided they had had too much dinner and not enough sleep. Merima said Ante also had had too much wine. They kissed us double and triple and quadruple. I thanked them both for the lovely dinner. Ana and her parents exchanged some words that I did not understand. A final "Ciao" and they were gone.

Ana and I opted for a cup of coffee instead of dessert.

"You've got great parents."

"Yeah, I think so," Ana sighed. "I just wish that I could see them more often then I do. I miss them so much."

I understood. "Family is important. Sometimes, at the end of the day, they are all you have."

For Croatians, Ana explained, having a close family is one of the most important and essential elements of life. Ante risked his own life to keep his family together, to keep them safe. There are no words for that.

For country folks, I explained, a sense of family and community is as normal as breathing and just as necessary. We agreed – sometimes, family is simply what you make it. Family is who you choose, too.

*   *   *

Basketball at the bomb shelter school was Ana's physical outlet for her frustration. Her favorite position was point guard because she was a good shooter. In the early months of 1994, she developed a dry cough that wouldn't leave. During the basketball games, Ana was getting weak and tired quickly. She often asked her coach to take her out of the game. The nearest pediatrician, Nora Milic, was seven miles outside of Tuzla. Since Ante had sold the car, Merima walked her daughter to her office.

Nora's preliminary tests included using a penlight to scan Ana's eyes and a tongue depressor to see her throat. She looked into her nose and ears, and thumped different areas on her thin body. These tests revealed no abnormalities. Both the doctor and Merima believed it was a case of the flu or a little cold. But Ana could not stop coughing and she wasn't regaining any strength, even with bed rest. Within a month, she could not even the climb stairs to their apartment.

Merima walked and even carried her daughter back to Nora Milic. The X-rays were useless. The doctor scanned the film as best she could but could not detect any problems. The clinic had suffered damages during the war. There was no money or mechanic available to fix the broken machine. The doctor made a note on the report that the machine had been broken for months and that the tests simply were not conclusive. Other minor tests were performed in the incapacitated office. Nothing came back with any certainty or clarity. Nora referred Merima and Ana to an adult internist near Tuzla.

Meanwhile, Ante was back in Croatia searching for a way to get his family out of the war. He had been gone for three months. There was no contact between Ante and Merima so she was not able to share the dilemma of Ana's condition with him.

Ana visited the internist on a Friday. She sat uncomfortably on the examination table while Merima stood by. The internist came, and Ana's nervousness was eased when she saw that the doctor was a woman. They discussed Ana's symptoms as the internist placed her hand on Ana's lower neck.

"Feel this," said the internist to her assistant. "The lump is like a stone."

Ana burst into tears. Even in Croatian, the word "lump" is interpreted as cancer.

"Don't get all worried just yet, we don't know anything for sure. Let's do some tests." Ana quieted. She had blood drawn and was scheduled for a biopsy on Monday morning. The waiting began.

That weekend Ana touched and pushed on the lump in her neck a thousand times over. She stood in front of the bathroom mirror examining herself each night. She wondered if the stone was cancer.

Merima walked to the internist's office to get the results from Ana's biopsy and blood tests. Her blood work was extremely abnormal. The biopsy revealed the worst – a malignant tumor. Merima cried and walked the streets of Tuzla for an hour before returning home. Ante had not been in touch for weeks and, for him, she also feared the worst. She could not face her beautiful children. She could not bear the sight of Ana's little neck. What was she to do? How would she save her family? Before she got home, she buried the paper with the hideous results in her purse.

A week later, Ana rummaged through her mother's pocketbook. She knew her mother was keeping something from her and she was determined to find out what it was. Ana wanted her results; she wanted to know why she was sick. When she got to the bottom of the purse, she found a crinkled piece of paper. She read her lab report. The confirmed result was cancer – Hodgkin's lymphoma Stage 2A. She took the paper to her mother and asked her to explain it to her. Merima dropped down onto the sofa; she was tired of being scared of death. "Oh, my little Ana, come here," she whispered and touched the sofa next to her. "I'll explain it to you."

Ana realized her mother was breaking down. There was no hospital in Bosnia for Ana to receive the specialized treatment she needed in her advanced state. Finally, when Ante was able to contact his family, Merima related the horrible news. Ana would die if she stayed in Tuzla.

Ante instructed his wife to sell everything they owned – the house, their furniture, their clothes, anything. From his end in Croatia, he was able to negotiate a hospital stay for Ana through an American agency that sponsored children of the war. Ante knew he had to get his family out of Bosnia. Merima sold everything and begged for more money. In total, they raised close to four thousand American dollars. It was just enough to secure them proper identification and seats on another secret bus.

The trip to Zagreb – Croatia's capital – took only two days, and Ana was growing sicker and weaker with each day. At the bus station, Merima and the children greeted Ante. The reunion was short; Ana was rushed to the hospital where she was directly admitted to one of the best facilities in the capital.

That was in May of 1994.

Ante obtained a sponsorship for his daughter through the International Rescue Committee; it paid almost all of her medical expenses in the capital. Zagreb was well protected from the war, but it was not immune. News of the Serbian attacks on Bosnia occupied nearly all of the conversations; but, for the Lipic family,

Zagreb, Croatia offered more protection than they had known in two years.

In Zagreb, Ana received immediate specialized care. Many American doctors worked in the capital and serviced the hospital. Since she was already in an advanced stage of the cancer, doctors gave her a 60% chance of survival. The first course of chemotherapy began within days. Inside the hospital, Ana was virtually isolated from the war, but her parents who lived a few blocks down heard the talk in the streets and in the stores. Serbia was not giving up, and ironically, neither was Ana.

She kept a journal, and each day she noted how many white blood cells she had, how much chemotherapy she had received, and the names and goings-on of the other children who were cancer patients. Ana, doing her best to prepare for her future doctor days, wrote down each chemical she received and the exact dosage. Each day, the medication was recorded, and for those drugs that contained English words, she asked the doctors to pronounce them for her. She knew exactly what medicines she was to receive, how much, and when. She asked her doctors for lengthy explanations of what the medicines were doing inside her body.

In the margins of the journals, she cut out pictures of beautiful models with fit bodies and long hair and pasted them next to her scientific entries.

There was a baby in Ana's ward, a twelve-month old girl named Elena who had been at the hospital for weeks before Ana arrived. The baby had leukemia and the nursing staff didn't allow the parents to visit. Even the smallest amount of bacteria could throw the baby's health into a downward spiral.

Ana took to the little baby on her floor. She had undergone radiation and because the two shared the same environment, she was essentially free of anything that might harm the baby. She was allowed to sit with the baby and even take care of her sometimes while the nurses went on lunch breaks.

Every day during her stay, she sat with baby Elena. Ana did her best to comfort the weak little body. She explained to her what was happening to them and why they couldn't see their parents.

Merima and Ante were allowed to visit their daughter once or twice a week. Ante visited less frequently than Merima because he was working overtime trying to make enough money to pay all their bills. When they came to visit, they never spoke of the war or news from Bosnia; Ana had her own battle to fight. The war would not impose on her there.

The hospital staff kept Ana and her parents mostly separated because she was still so susceptible to bacteria and viruses, but Merima Lipic was completely devoted to her sick child and never missed a visiting day. Little Tomislav came when he could, but his parents had enrolled him in a music school where he studied the piano all day. Ana heard her mother talk about Tomislav's amazing proficiency and his rumored genius. This came as no surprise to his big sister because she knew Tomislav was more special than anyone realized.

One day, Ana felt a lump on her left side. She called for the nurses and doctors.

"Ana, it feels like your rib."

"No, but this really hurts."

Doctors poked and pushed on the lump. Ana insisted that something was wrong, that something did not feel right. Finally, her doctor scheduled her for an ultra-sound.

She lay quietly on the bed and stared with all her intensity at the tiny black and white television screen. The doctor rolled the jellied instrument across the lump. Ana winced in pain and the doctor scrunched his face up and got close to the computer screen.

"Miss Lipic, that lump is your rib."

Embarrassment washed over her face. She looked at her doctor and said, "I'm really sorry about this, but you know, it does feel like something."

For Ana, life in the hospital was a series of small survivals. She saw each new pain or bump as an ominous indicator of the end. Reassurances were often meaningless because, in her gut, Ana knew that something was getting worse. Her intuition was all she needed, and within a few weeks, she proved the doctors wrong.

Complications arose and doctors upgraded her condition to a Stage B. She was put in isolation for two weeks. The red chemotherapy began; red makes your hair fall out. At 14 years old, losing her beautiful blonde hair was beyond comprehension. She tried to fight the inevitable. Ana refused to wash or brush her hair in the days following the red chemotherapy. But once it started to fall, Ana panicked. In less than a week, she was completely bald. More and more models with long hair began to appear in the margins of Ana's diary. Merima cried for days and nights; Ante could not bear to watch.

The second course of chemotherapy was the triumph.

By November of 1994, Ana had beaten the cancer. She could leave the hospital, and the doctors told her that her hair would come back soon. Ana's recovery had to be monitored for the next five years to ensure a complete remission. If the cancer resurfaced in that time, she needed to have the technology and the medicine available to restart her treatments. But Ante did not trust the boundaries of the war; Serbia kept pressing the lines forward into Croatia. He contacted Ana's sponsorship agency; they offered to maintain her status at Hershey Medical Center in Hershey, Pennsylvania in the United States. Ante gathered his family and told them that the only way they could ensure Ana stayed well was to move to America. The Lipic family did not speak English. Merima and Ante had no money. Ana and Tomislav did not know where Pennsylvania was.

No one knew what they would do, but Ante assured his family of one thing: they would survive.

*   *   *

"Do you want to know what my parents said to me before they left?" Ana asked me.

"Sure, if you want to tell me." I took a sip of coffee, French Vanilla creamer and more sugar than it needed.

She smiled wide like her parents. "We are going home, home to Croatia for a visit."

"Ana, that's great! I bet you can't wait to go."

"I have not seen my family in seven years. When we left after my cancer, we never went back. I don't know what anyone looks like anymore."

As I listened, I realized that I have never thought of my life in those terms. My entire family lives within thirty miles of each other – aunts, uncles, cousins, and grandparents, even the extended relations. All Ana had here was her mother, her father, and her brother. That was all. I wondered what my life would have been like with only three family members. Whether it was right or wrong, I was thankful that I had never known such circumstances.

Ana often shined a bright light on my life. I had never been hungry nor without basic necessities nor my family. Yet my comfortable life was never the focus of our discussions. All my life examinations were my own – never once did Ana judge me for not having suffered the hardships that she faced. Ana only pitied me for never having seen the Adriatic. When we talked, the focus was always on our similarities: strong relationships with parents and siblings, a love of the ocean, a relaxed way of life, and the vital importance of telling the truth, being loyal, and always trying to do the right thing.

"I'm a little scared actually. Nothing will look like it did and no one will be the same." Ana said.

"But maybe that's why you have to go back. You need to see the differences so you can make peace within yourself."

"I have to figure out where my home is. I've been in America since 1994, but I know I left a part of me in Croatia and in Bosnia."

"One day, Ana, you'll find your place." I hoped that I was right.

Ana thought for a while and then she said, "I wonder if my cousin still has my old stuffed animal, Monkey. I gave him to her before we left to go to Bosnia on the bus."

For the life of me, I could not say anything. Not a word.

We drank our coffee and ate animal crackers, and eventually, the subject changed, but we did not forget. How could I? Home is supposed to be a simple concept. It is the place where you live, where you sleep, where you find all the tangibles and intangibles of everyday living. All of my life, I knew my home was a barn-shaped house in the country on the outskirts of Salisbury, Maryland. My place in the world was secure because I could point to a physical structure or a spot on a map and say without sadness, "That's where I live. That's my home."

* * *

On November 17, 1994, Ana stepped off the plane and touched her feet on American soil. The only English words she held in her vocabulary were "yes", "no", "soup", and a few random curse words. Lancaster, Pennsylvania would be her new home.

Ana was enrolled into a parochial school. The nuns gave her numerous math and language tests. She scored well on the math tests but miserably failed on the English tests. They placed her in the 10th grade and gave her a uniform.

On the first day of class, Ana was lost in a foreign place. The language did not make sense, the people stared at her uncovered head, and her life was thousands of miles away. The teacher would come by her desk and turn her book to the page they were reading. He pointed to the words and had her follow his finger.

Ana returned to basketball, but this time there was a large gym with overhead lighting and uniforms for the girls. There was a wooden floor with lines permanently painted on the floor. She did not understand the coach nor the other girls, but she knew how to shoot the ball. The coach put her on the team and for the first time that day, Ana was happy. Despite the language barrier and the threats of the fragility of remission, she tried harder than anyone on the team.

When she went home, the small television was kept on mute all the time; the Lipic family watched it in closed caption. Over time, they linked words to objects. A nun had given Ana some picture-word books left over from the elementary grades, and she had brought them home to share with her family. She and Tomislav would stare at the picture of a cat and look at the letters "c-a-t." On the lines below, they wrote, "cat" five times and tried to say it out loud. Picture books and closed caption television: Ana learned to speak functional English in three and a half months.

One day, her mother came back from the mailbox and handed Ana a strange yellow envelope. The return address was Zagreb, Croatia. Instantly curious and scared, her fingers slid under the seal and pulled out a small letter. It was from one of the doctors on her cancer floor, and the letter was to inform her that baby Elena had died of complications. The news threw Ana into her mother's arms and into a fit of tears, sickness, and homesickness. But for which home and which country?

Merima stroked her daughter's fuzzy head while Ana's face remained buried in her mother's chest. Where would home be now? In that town called Harrisburg where people laughed at her bald head? In this America where people talked in strange hard syllables that flew by too quickly? Ana knew nothing except that she felt lost.

In her Latin class at the parochial school, students were asked to pick names. Ana chose Elena. Honoring the little one was the best she could do from her place in time and distance.

*   *   *

The Lipic family traveled home to Croatia and Bosnia on Christmas Day in 2000. The eight-hour flight tired everyone on the plane, except for their anxious family. Returning home was the first step towards healing their hearts and smoothing their scars.

Merima and Ante wanted to see and touch their brothers and sisters, nieces and nephews. Ante wanted to hug and kiss his mother; Merima needed to put fresh flowers on her mother's grave.

Tomislav dreamed to see Europe through a young artist's eyes. He longed for a scholarship to Oxford to study classical piano because, as life had turned out, Tomislav was a musical genius with talents that far exceeded anyone's expectations of a young boy from a war-torn nation. Before he began his future studies, he wanted to see again with new eyes the places his Bosnian cousins already knew and loved.

Ana needed to make peace with her present fears and her old life. She longed to swim in the Adriatic Sea near the beaches of her old home in Split. She dreamed of lying on her back and drifting to the easy rolling waves and gentle pull of the currents. She wanted to see those cliffs and caves she had often explored with her brother. Times had changed, she knew, but this place would always be the calm before her storms, the peace before the war. The warmth of the sea washed over her as she smiled up at the sky – her eyes perfectly matching the sea.

While in Croatia, Ana re-introduced herself to the children from the neighborhood. The boys were now men with jobs working the waters – fishermen, sailors, and ship builders. The girls had become beautiful women who carried Croatian babies in their bellies and laughed as they recalled the games they played. The olive and grape vineyards belonged to different families now, but the smell of their ripe husks was as she remembered, but had almost forgotten.

These small villages were close-knit communities. Everyone knew everybody. Life was not easy and the war had left most of the Balkan states poor, even the villages far away from it, like Split and Hvar, felt the economic strain on goods and services. To send a package to the United States from Croatia required a week's worth of a worker's wages. Clothing was an expensive commodity. Ana left almost all her clothing with her cousins and they marveled at names like "GAP" and "L.L. Bean". Ana was so exotic!

She contacted Nora Milic, the doctor who first discovered her cancer. They reunited over a big dinner at the doctor's home in Tuzla. "I knew you would survive," Nora Milic said to her over full glasses of wine. "If anyone were to make it through the war, the cancer, and the move to America, I knew it would be little Ana."

When she returned to the states, she called me. Her voice was light and she sounded happier, refreshed even. I asked her if she found peace and closure, and Ana said she found out where her home was.

"Where?" I was eager to know.

"Maryland," she said.

"Seriously?" I had expected her to say that Croatia and Bosnia would always be home to her.

"Well, Croatia and Bosnia will always be a part of me. It will always be my home, but so much time has passed and I've changed so much."

I listened as she continued: "I've been in Maryland for several years now. I feel comfortable and I know the different places around here. But this is my home now."

And she was right. Ana navigates Baltimore and Annapolis much better than I do and the look on her face when she's on the waters of the Chester River or the Atlantic is the same look as a true blood of the Shore. She knows more geography and places in Maryland than I ever learned. Then it occurred to me. Ana picked Maryland as her home. This was her choice.

"You know what else is funny?"

"What?"

"People on the Eastern Shore are just like the people from back home."

I almost knew what she was about to say.

"You all are a relaxed and friendly type of people: the watermen we see down on the river; the people who sell tomatoes and watermelons on the roadside; you and your family."

"I know what you mean. Maybe it's because we live in a beautiful place – we can't help but be nice."

"Exactly, well, the Chesapeake Bay is not the Adriatic Sea, but people in Croatia open up their homes to you. When you are a guest, they say, 'Anything of mine is yours.' And they mean it. Your parents are like that when I go to your house. Eastern Shore people are warm and nice. They open up to you."

After I hung up the phone, I thought about Ana, one of the greatest friends I'd ever had. Ana: the girl who would not die in a frozen bus; the cancer patient who would not surrender to cancer; the refugee who would not break under pressure as an American transplant. That she refused to die and refused to be left behind reminds me that her story is more than I can truly understand. While I faced the schoolyard bully and pre-algebra, she faced the almost certain death of childhood cancer. While I held my sister's hand in evening thunderstorms, she clutched her brother in a shower of bombs.

While I lived, she survived.

*   *   *

To protect Ana and her family and to preserve their privacy, I changed their names, but this does not alter their story. She is here among the tales of crabbers and farmers because she is the same as the rest of us. With a stranger's eyes, Ana found comfort and similarity between her old home and her new one and those connections are real and striking. She is a lover of Maryland; after thousands of miles and memories, she chose this as her home.

I had always held the belief that Eastern Shore folk are a strange breed and, as such, perhaps we are difficult to love. That belief was shattered when I met Ana Lipic. After listening to her story, I was instantly grateful for my childhood – growing up on the quiet and beautiful Delmarva Peninsula. She lived inside of a war while I watched its images on television. I had a choice to look away. She did not. And I know the war changed her in ways that make my narration of it suspicious.

Years have passed since our college days in Chestertown. I will always be thankful for those years spent at Washington College and for the time I spent with my friend. We find ourselves as adults, facing a world full of challenges and pitfalls and wonderful surprises. This story does not end here. It cannot end here.

Ana has a family of her own now, a husband and two beautiful children. She remains a lover of the Eastern Shore. Her children roam the sandy beaches; they squeal with delight as foamy breakers wash over their toes and laugh as sand crabs wriggle in their chubby hands. Ana smiles as she watches them, reassured in the knowledge that this is a place for her children, a place for all of God's children.

SOURCE LISTS

THE CURSE OF FRANKLIN

Brown, Leonard. Personal Interview. 25 July 2001.

Ellis, Edwin L. "A Glimpse of the Early History of the Eastern Shore of Virginia." Old Home Prize Essay. June 1920.

"Fire Destroys Franklin City Methodist Church." Peninsula Enterprise 21 Feb.1941.

"Franklin City ... Swept Out!" The Democratic Messenger 23 May 1896.

Gunter, Benjamin T. Deed. 2 March 1880.

Jester, Dora and Naomi Mason. "History of Greenbackville and Franklin City." 1967. Unpublished article via Methodist Protestant Church of Greenbackville archives.

John R. Franklin. Photograph. Nabb Research Center, Salisbury, Maryland.

Jones, Garland. Personal Interview. December 2000.

Jones, Mabel. Personal Interviews. December 2000 & April 2001.

Mariner, Kirk. <u>Nothing Ever Happened in Arcadia</u>. Richmond, Virginia: Cooper-Trent Printers, April 1968.

---. <u>Once Upon an Island: The History of Chincoteague</u>. New Church, Virginia: Miona Publications, 1996.

---. Letter to the author. January 2001.

Marshall, Ginger. Personal Interview. 21 February 2002.

<u>Native Americans</u>. Chart. Chincoteague National Wildlife Refuge, Tom's Cove Visitor Center.

Ryan, John. "Recalling Ghost Town's Boom." <u>The Daily Times</u> 16 January 1981: 5.

Shockley, Ted. "Franklin City: The Eastern Shore's Ghost Town." <u>The Eastern Shore News</u> 11 August 1993.

Tarr, Mae. Personal Interviews. September 2000 through April 2001.

Time Table of the Pennsylvania Railroad. January 31, 1926. 2nd Edition.

Truitt, Reginald V., and Millard G. Les Callette. <u>Worcester County: Maryland's Arcadia</u>. Baltimore, Maryland: Waverly Press, 1977.

Union United Methodist Church. "Union UMC Homecoming 1877-1999: 122 Years Young." October 17, 1999.

United States. Bureau of the Census. <u>Census Report of 1850, Worcester County</u>.

---. <u>Census Report of 1860, Worcester County</u>.

---. <u>Census Report of 1870, Worcester County</u>.

<u>Unknown Name of Picture/Artist</u>. Oyster and Maritime Museum, Chincoteague Island, Virginia.

Whitelaw, Ralph T. <u>Virginia's Eastern Shore</u>. Vol. 2. Camden, Maine: Picton Press, 1989. 2 vols.

And Justice For All

"2nd Man Tried In Stockton Case." The Salisbury Times 31 July 1940: 1.

"Bats And Fenceposts Used Against Police, O'Conor Says." The Salisbury Times 14 Feb 1940: 1, 5.

"Collick And Manuel Are Indicted For Pilchard Murder." The Worcester Democrat. Date Unknown.

"Collick Given Death For Slaying." The Salisbury Times 1 Aug 1940: 1.

"Collick, Manuel Plead Innocent." The Salisbury Times 14 Mar 1940: 1, 3.

"Collick Pays With Life For Shore Murder." The Salisbury Times 13 Aug 1940: 1-2.

"Collick Put In Death Row At State Pen." The Salisbury Times 2 Aug 1940: 1.

"Collick Told Girl Of Slaying." The Salisbury Times 30 July 1940: 1-2.

"Collick Tried In Pilchard Case." The Salisbury Times 29 July 1940:1.

"Collick Will Be Hanged on Friday, 13th." The Salisbury Times 8 Aug 1940: 1.

"Damage Is Heavy In Shore Blizzard." The Salisbury Times 15 Feb 1940: 1.

Ellison, Ralph. Invisible Man. New York: Vintage International, 1980.

"Funeral For Slain Farmer At Girdletree." The Democratic Messenger 15 Feb 1940: 1.

"Grand Jury Indicts Collick And Manuel For Murder." The Democratic Messenger. Date Unknown.

"Harvey W. Pilchard Murdered – His Wife Shot." The Democratic Messenger 15 Feb 1940: 1, 8.

"His Own Dog Aids Capture of Fugitive." Unknown newspaper. 16 Feb 1940: 1,2.

"Homes Are Searched For Slayer." The Salisbury Times 15 Feb 1940: 1.

Howard, Judy. Personal Interview. January 2001.

"Hunt Two For Worcester Murder." The Salisbury Times 12 Feb 1940: 1.

Jones, Jacqueline. Personal Interview. April 2001.

"Judges Confer on Stockton Murder." The Salisbury Times 17 Feb 1940: 1.

Kerbin, William Jr. Personal Interview. January 2001.

McDonnell, Owen F. "Suspect Accuses Friend In Slaying." Inquirer: n/a.

"Mob Leaders Who Seized Negro Women Known, Sheriff Says." The Salisbury Times 14 Feb 1940: 1,5.

"Murder – Robbery – Rape Committed At Stockton By Negroes Sun. Night." The Worcester Democrat 16 Feb 1940:1, 12.

"No Date Set For Slaying Arraignment." The Salisbury Times 28 Feb 1940: 1.

"Pilchard Case May Be Heard In Early June." The Salisbury Times 15 May 1940: 1-2.

"Shore Murder Suspect Held." The Salisbury Times 16 Feb 1940: 1.

"Slaying Suspect Shot In Woods." The Salisbury Times 13 Feb 1940: 1-2.

"Stockton Case Prisoners In Towson Jail." The Salisbury Times 13 Mar 1940: 1.

Stump, Brice. "The Country Lawyer." The Daily Times. 7 Jan 2001: E1, E3.

Tarr, Mae. Personal Interview. December 2000.

"Trouble On The Shore." <u>The Baltimore Evening Sun</u>. 15 Feb 1940.

"Worcester Jury Recalled On Stockton Murder." <u>The Salisbury Times</u> 19 Feb 1940: 1.

SONS OF THE CHESAPEAKE

"400 Attend Last Rites For Nelson." The Salisbury Times 9 July 1949: 1,2.

"Accomack Co. Grand Jury Finds No True Bill Against Acree." The Peninsula Enterprise 16 Aug 1949.

"Acree Decision Irks Crisfield." The Salisbury Times 16 July 1949: 1.

"Acree Hearing Is Set For August 5th." Marylander and Herald 29 July 1949: 1.

"Acree Held in Jail, $10,000 Bond Withdrawn." The Salisbury Times 8 July 1949: 1.

"Acree Was Never On Virginia's Payroll." The Salisbury Times 9 July 1949: 1.

Bailey, Hon. Levin Claude. "Maryland's Boundary Controversies." 22 June 1951.

"Boy Hears Father Shot, Goes To See For Himself." The Salisbury Times 6 July 1949: 1.

"Chesapeake Bay Tragedy Focuses National Attention On Old Bi-State Problem." The Peninsula Enterprise Date unknown.

Clark, Charles B. "The Eastern Shore of Maryland and Virginia." Vol. 1.

"Compact of 1785" Report and Journal of the Joint Commission to Adjust the Boundary. 1872

"Crisfield Man Fatally Shot in Tangier Sound." The Salisbury Times 5 July 1949: 1.

"Crisfield Takes Day To Mourn, Rites Held For Slain Crabber." The Salisbury Times 8 July 1949: 1.

"Crisfield Watermen Resent Shooting Of Fellow-Neighbor." The Salisbury Times 6 July 1949: 1.

Dize, Fran. Personal Interview. February 2002.

"Extradition Of Acree Is Asked." The Salisbury Times 22 July 1949: 1,2.

"Extradition Of Acree is Sought." The Salisbury Times 16 July 1949: 1.

Fowler, Jacqueline. Personal Interview. September 2001-April 2001.

"Gov. Lane Joines Probe Of Shore Crabber's Death." The Salisbury Times 11 July 1949: 1.

"Grand Jury Gets Acree Charge Today." The Salisbury Times 15 Aug 1949: 1.

"Grand Jury Indicts David Acree On Murder Charge." Marylander and Herald 30 Sept 1949: 1.

Horton, Tom. Article in Baltimore Sun. 8 March 1981.

"Latest Tragedy In Chesapeake Points To Past Bay Conflicts." The Peninsula Enterprise 8 July 1949.

Nelson, Royce. Personal Interview. February-April 2001.

"Norfolk Fishermen Condemn Shooting Of Crisfield Man." The Salisbury Times 9 July 1949: 1.

"Slaying Issue Still Unsettled." The Salisbury Times 14 July 1949: 1,3.

Tawes, Scorchy. Personal Interview. July 2002.

"Tuck Asks: 'No Hurried Judgment' In Shooting." The Salisbury Times 14 July 1949: 3.

"Two States Probe Crabber's Death." The Salisbury Times 6 July 1949: 1.

Tyler, Carl "Ky". Personal Interview. July 2001.

"Va. Authorities Refuse Surrender Of Officers In Conservation Killing." Marylander and Herald 8 July 1949: 1.

"Va Frees Crabber's Slayer." The Salisbury Times 16 Aug 1949: 1,2.

"Va. Governor Refuses Acree Extradition." <u>Marylander and Herald</u> 12 Aug 1949: 1.

"Va. Holds Crabber's Slayer." <u>The Salisbury Times</u> 7 July 1949: 1.

"Va. Will Try Acree In August." <u>The Salisbury Times</u> 13 July 1949: 1.

"Va Won't Give Up Acree." <u>The Salisbury Times</u> 6 Aug 1949: 1,2.

"Virginia Acts To Try Acree For Murder." <u>Marylander and Herald</u> 15 July 1949: 1.

Wennersten, John R. <u>The Oyster Wars of Chesapeake Bay</u>. Centreville, Maryland: Tidewater Publishers: 1981.

Wilson, Woodrow T. <u>History of Crisfield and Surrounding Areas on Maryland's Eastern Shore</u>. Baltimore, Maryland: Gateway Press, 1973.

A Forgotten History

African-American Inventor Series. Laws. 11 June 2002. <www.ehhs.cmich.edu/~rlandrum/laws.htm>

American RadioWorks. Remembering Jim Crow: Laws. June 2002. <www.americanradioworks.org/features/remembering/laws.html>

Anderson, Margaret L. "Discovering the Past / Considering the Future: Lessons from the Eastern Shore." A History of African Americans of Delaware and Maryland's Eastern Shore. Ed.

"Anti-Segregation Wins Good Press." Salisbury Times 19 May 1954: 1.

Ash, Louise. Hickory Stick to Computer Chip: A history of public education in Worcester County. Salisbury, Maryland: Printery, Inc. 1992.

"Baltimore Head Sees No School Troubles." Salisbury Times 18 May 1954: 1

Berlin, Ira. ed. Freedom: A documentary history of Emancipation 1861-1867. Series II: The Black Military

Experience. New York: Cambridge University Press, 1982.

Corddrey, George H. Wicomico County History. Salisbury, Maryland: Peninsula Press, 1981.

"Court Plannning on Segregation Hearing Oct. 12." Salisbury Times 19 May 1954: 1,8.

Crippin, Charles. Personal Interview. 1 July 2002.

Dalleo, Peter T. "The Growth of Delaware's Antebellum Free African American Community." A History of African Americans of Delaware and Maryland's Eastern Shore. Ed. Carole C. Marks.

Davis, Theodore J. Jr. "Socioeconomic Change: A Community in Transition." A History of African Americans of Delaware and Maryland's Eastern Shore. Ed. Carole C. Marks.

"Delaware Plans School Parley." Salisbury Times 18 May 1954: 1, 10.

"Douglass, Frederick." Microsoft Encarta Online Encyclopedia 2002. <http://encarta.msn.com> 12 June 2002.

Gatling, Sudie. Personal Interview. 28 June 2002 and March 2007.

Gibson, Judith Y. "Mighty Oaks: Five Black Educators." A History of African Americans of

Delaware and Maryland's Eastern Shore. Ed. Carole C. Marks.

Guy, Anita Aidt. Maryland's Persistent Pursuit to End Slavery, 1850-1864. Ed. Graham Hodges. New York: Garland Publishing, Inc., 1997.

Harris, Claire. Personal Interview. 8 August 2002.

Harris, Melvin. Personal Interview. 8 August 2002.

Hopwood, Joseph E. "A Note on the Socio-Cultural History of the Black Communities of Wetipquin and Tyaskin." Friends of Bannaker-Douglass Museum, Annapolis, Maryland. 11 Dec. 1993.

Mariner, Kirk. Once Upon an Island: The History of Chincoteague. New Church, Virginia: Miona Publications, 1996.

Marks, Carole C. 4 August 1997. University of Delaware. 11 June 2002. <www.udel.edu/BlackHistory/discoveringthepast.html>

"Marland Expects Little Trouble in W. Va." Salisbury Times 18 May 1954: 1.

Marlow, James. "NAACP To Fight Now Against Other Segregations." Salisbury Times 18 May 1954.

"Marshall, Thurgood." Microsoft Encarta Online Encyclopedia 2002. <http://encarta.msn.com> 12 June 2002.

Martin, Abagail. "Caught in the Middle: The Civil War on the Eastern Shore." 19 March 1990. Old Home Prize Essay.

Martin Luther King, Jr. National Historic Site Interpretive Staff. "Jim Crow Laws" 5 Jan. 1998. National Historical Site. May 2002. <www.nps.gov/malu/documents/jim_crow_laws.htm>

"Maryland To Await Court's Decrees on Segregation End." <u>Salisbury Times</u> 27 May 1954: 1, 8.

Morgan, Philip D. <u>Slave Counterpoint: Black Culture in the Eighteenth Century Chesapeake & Lowcountry</u>. Chapel Hill, North Carolina: University of North Carolina Press, 1998.

Newton, James E. "Black Americans in Delaware: An Overview." <u>A History of African Americans of Delaware and Maryland's Eastern Shore</u>. Ed. Carole C. Marks.

<u>Remembering Jim Crow</u>. Minnesota Public Radio & NPR News. American RadioWorks.

Roe, Megan. "Bringing the Shore Together: The Integration of Schools." 19 February 1991. Old Home Prize Essay.

Rollo, Vera. <u>The Negro in Maryland: A Short History</u>. Lanham, Maryland: Maryland Historical Press, 1972.

"Salisburian Hears Anti-Segregation Ruling." <u>Salisbury Times</u> 18 May 1954: 1.

"Segregation End to be Discussed." Salisbury Times 27 May 1954: 1.

Schoettler, Carl. "Tracing Maryland's 'Invisible' Black Civil War Soldiers." Baltimore Evening Sun. 11 June 1990.

"School Segregation End Seen Months or Years Away." Salisbury Times 18 May 1954: 1, 10.

Small, Clara L. "Abolitionists, Free Blacks, and Runaway Slaves: Surviving Slavery on Maryland's Eastern Shore." A History of African Americans of Delaware and Maryland's Eastern Shore. Ed. Carole C. Marks.

"State Bides Time on Segregation End." Salisbury Times 19 May 1954: 1.

State of Maryland. Works Projects Administration, Writer's Program. Maryland: A Guide to the Old Line State. New York: Oxford University Press, 1940.

"States Face Vast Problems After Courts Anti-Segregation Edict." Salisbury Times 18 May 1954.

Stump, Brice. "Graduation Day." Daily Times 17 May 2002.

"Tubman, Harriett Ross." Microsoft Encarta Online Encyclopedia 2002 <http://encarta.msn.com> 12 June 2002.

United States. National Archives. Letters to the Bureau of Refuges, Freedmen, and Abandoned Lands. Records for the State of Maryland and Delaware. 20 June 2002.

"Virginia Governor To Call Conference." <u>Salisbury Times</u> 18 May 1954: 1.

Wennersten, John R. <u>Maryland's Eastern Shore: A Journey in Time and Place</u>. Centreville, Maryland: Tidewater Press, 1992.

---. <u>Tidewater Somerset: 1850-1970</u>.

Wennersten, Ruth Ellen. "The Historical Evolution of a Black Land Grant College, University of Maryland, Eastern Shore, 1886-1970." Diss. University of Maryland Eastern Shore, 1976.

Wicomico County Retired Teacher's Association. <u>Recollections: Wicomico's One Room Schools</u>. 1977.

Wilson, Woodrow T. <u>History of Crisfield and Surrounding Areas on Maryland's Eastern Shore</u>. Baltimore, Maryland: Gateway Press, 1973.

ANA'S STORY

"Croatia." Microsoft® Encarta® Online Encyclopedia 2001 http://encarta.msn.com © 1997-2001 Microsoft Corporation. All rights reserved.

Lipic, Ana. Personal Interviews. September 2000-April 2001 and March 2007.

Lipic, Ante. Personal Interview. October 2000.

Lipic, Merima. Personal Interview. October 2000.

"Sarajevo Olympic Games" The Eighties Server, a division of MacroMusic, Inc. Copyright 2002. <http://www.eighties.com/Entertainment/Sports/Olympics/1984/winter.html>

Why Bosnia? Writings on the Balkan War. Editors Rabia Ali & Lawrence Lifschultz. The Pamphleteer's Press, Inc. Stony Creek, Connecticut. Copyright 1993. Sections used: *A Chronology*, pgs 341-347.

Zlata's Diary. A Child's Life in Sarajevo. Zlata Filipović. Introduction: Janine DiGiovanni. Translated by Christina Pribichevich-Zorić. Viking Penguin. New York. Copyright 1994.